T0116818

I Don't Look like Where I've Been

This is my life and testimony

Margaret L. Lively

iUniverse, Inc.
Bloomington

I Don't Look like Where I've Been
This is my life and testimony

Copyright © 2011 Margaret L. Lively

All rights reserved. No part of this book may be used or reproduced by any means,
graphic, electronic, or mechanical, including photocopying, recording, taping or by any
information storage retrieval system without the written permission of the publisher
except in the case of brief quotations embodied in critical articles and reviews.

iUniverse books may be ordered through booksellers or by contacting:

iUniverse
1663 Liberty Drive
Bloomington, IN 47403
www.iuniverse.com
1-800-Authors (1-800-288-4677)

Because of the dynamic nature of the Internet, any Web addresses or links contained in
this book may have changed since publication and may no longer be valid. The views
expressed in this work are solely those of the author and do not necessarily reflect the
views of the publisher, and the publisher hereby disclaims any responsibility for them.

Any people depicted in stock imagery provided by Thinkstock are models,
and such images are being used for illustrative purposes only.

Certain stock imagery © Thinkstock.

ISBN: 978-1-4502-2653-0 (pbk)
ISBN: 978-1-4502-2654-7 (ebk)

Printed in the United States of America

iUniverse rev. date: 2/16/2011

1.

GROWING UP AS A CHILD

I WAS BORN IN Oxberry Mississippi, on a very small Farm. We lived about thirty five miles from the town of Grenada Mississippi and ten miles from Holcomb. We had one little feed store where we could buy bread, candy, crackers, chicken feed, flour, meal sugar, block salt for the cows, bridles for the horses, and saddles. We would hitch the horses to the wagon and drive to Grenada for clothes and furniture. We never had to buy any meats. Most everybody raised and killed their own meats, and planted and raised their own vegetables. Slaughter time was in the fall of the year. We would always cage the animals and hand feed them a few months so that they would be cleaned out for the slaughter. If there were any families that were known not to have meat doing that season, everybody pitched in and supplied those families. They made sure everybody's needs were met with plenty of food. People loved and looked out for each other.

Nothing was thrown away. They even cleaned and washed the hog's guts and cook them, they are called chitterlings. They took the head of the hog cleaned it, grind it into mush, and made hoghead cheese.

We can purchase hoghead cheese and chitterlings in the meat markets today. The head cheese is very delicious, and taste like pickle meat. African Americans learned how to create and use these foods from slavery. That was what they could afford. They learned how to make them taste good. So today a lot of people still eat those foods not knowing they cause lots of diseases. Notice: I said they pinned the animals up and cleaned their insides out before they kill them. Chickens and hogs eat everything, so they must be put up in pens and feed only what we gave then to eat to clean them out. Everybody canned lots of fruits and vegetables. They canned jars by the hundreds, so when the winters came, they would open up those jars of food and make dinner. They were good nutritious fruits and vegetables. When our parents planted the gardens, and every thing was ripe, ready for picking, we kids would go into the gardens and eat lots of raw vegetables such as, green onions, tomatoes, and cucumbers. They planted fields of water melons and cantaloupes. And all types of vegetables. Everything was planted in March. When they ripen; usually in August; the farmers would hitch up the wagons and take wagon loads of melons, vegetables, and everything they raised into town to sell. People in the Towns and Cities were happy to see those wagons rolling down the streets, and hear those men yelling; "melons, Vegetables, Potatoes" and whatever they had on those wagons. When they returned everything has been sold. The prices were very reasonable.

We could drive down any road or highway and see all kinds of fruit trees, plum, peach, persimmon, and apple trees. Black berries were everywhere free for the picking. As major high ways were built, those trees slowly disappeared. The young people today don't have any idea what it would be like to see fruit trees every where beside the roads. We planted blue berries, cherries and grapes. Every body shared whatever they had. We raised turkeys, and Peacocks. Peacock is so beautiful when they spread their wings. They are all colors and look like a big fan.

My mother was from a family of seven, four boys and three girls. She was next to the oldest girl. When their mother lost her eye sight, my mother quit school to take care of her. Her oldest sister was married and lived away from home. Most of the responsibility fell on my mother. When my mother turned nineteen she still was not dating. You were considered an old maid if you were not married by age twenty. When my mother met my father he was forty and she had just turned twenty. People back then considered age forty very old. My father had just been released from prison for a murder he swears he did not commit. They got married right away. My mother said she was twenty when I was born. I could always know her age because she was twenty years older than me. I was their only child, the little girl that everybody wanted. My father had been married before. He had one daughter and two sons by his first wife before he went to prison. (More about them later)

My mother was very pretty she was tall with long flowing hair. Her mother was mixed with Indian (Seminole) my father was about five-nine and he was cripple. One leg was real small and he walked on the side of that small foot. The other leg was big and strong and he wore rubber boots because they were soft and easier to walk on the side of that foot.

When I was two years old; my mother taught me a riddle. It went like this. She would tickle my tummy, she would ask me; "**What's in the belly**" I'd say guts in the belly, she'd say; 'what's in the guts, I'd say shits in the guts. She would laugh, that was so funny to her. My mother taught all her niece's that riddle. She also taught me how to do a dance call **pull the skip**. I could really do that dance well. Whenever anybody would come over to visit us, they wanted to see me dance. I was not shy. To do that dance you put one foot out and pull your arms and body way back, and then the other foot. People would say to my parents; "she should be enrolled in a dance school". My mother never really wanted children so she didn't have anymore. She was hoping I would be a boy. My dad says, "He would come home from work and find me sitting in an orange crate box too close to the fire in front of the fire place. I would be trying to protect my neck from the heat. He would pull me away from the fire and scold my mother, but she would do it again and again. My dad said, "He was afraid that a spark from the fire would pop into the box and set the box on fire". He thought she was doing it on purpose. I think she was just trying to keep me warm. Those fire places only warmed the front of you while your back side would be freezing. That was the only heat everybody had those days. The front of the women's legs would be baked trying to get close enough to keep warm.

While I was still two years old, my mom accidentally stuck the corner of a cotton bold in her fore finger while picking cotton. Cotton bolds has sharp corners, and the cotton grows inside the bold. As you pull the cotton from the bold, you can very easy snag your finger. She let it go un-noticed until it became inflamed. Mother walked the floor at night moaning with the pain. My dad had to hitch up the wagon with the mules over in the night and take her to the Doctor. Doctor'

3

back then had their offices in their homes. He did surgery to remove the bone from her fore finger. She would often say, "I have one bone less than what I was born with". When I got older, we were talking about me remembering things when I was two years old. She said; "I don't believe you can remember things when you were that age". I told her about how she would walk the floor at night in pain with her finger, and everything about my dad taking her to the Doctor. She believed me and said that is exactly what happened.

Mrs. Lottie and her husband were friends of my parents. They would come to visit us, and Mrs. Lottie would beg my parents to give me to them. They had been married a few years and had not had any children. My mother would say if it's alright with her daddy its ok with me. But my dad would never answer her. It was not uncommon for people to give their children to friends those days. Mrs. Lottie would sit for hours begging my dad to answer her either yes or no; but he would remain silent. That's how he would ignore you. If he did not agree with you, you could follow him around all day he would not say a word..

Finally Mrs. Lottie got pregnant, she and her husband were very happy, every one was. She didn't live to raise her baby. She died a few days after the baby was born. I heard my parents say, the midwife said, "She did not bleed enough after the birth; she hemorrhaged after death. I was two and a half years old when she died. We missed her very much. I think she would have made a wonderful mother; even to me if my dad had said yes.

2.

Going to Live With My Grand Parents

WHEN I WAS THREE years of age I went to live with my grand parents.
They called my grandma Ms. Molly, and she called my grandpa Mr.
Paa. Grandma never saw me because she was blind when I was born. At
the age of three, I was old enough to lead her around. She needed me
to be her eyes. I loved my grand parents. They were farmers and moved
to many different farms. We were very poor for material things but rich
in love. We never owned our land so we would lease land from people
who own plantations. They would supply the farmers with money to
purchase the seeds to plant. At harvest time the farmers were to pay
back all the money and half of whatever their harvest came to be. Some
times the land would be too poor to harvest a good crop. The next year
or two we would move to another plantation. My grandma became ill
and soon was bed ridden. My favorite Auntie was still living at home,
but she worked with my Grandpa in the fields.

When I turned four years old I had the full responsibility of watching
and helping Grandma. My job was to make sure the flies didn't crawl on
her. She would take Epsom salts to control her blood pressure; she would
spill some of the salts into the bed. I liked the taste of these Epsom salts, so
when she spilled them I would be up in the bed with her eating the salts.
Granny had to continue reminding me to fan the flies because I would get
distracted and be playing. I would forget what I should be doing. When
she got tired of telling me the same thing day after day, she told grandpa
when he got in from the field that she had to keep reminding me to fan

the flies. He did a little scolding, and went out to get a switch off the tree to give me a whipping. Auntie hid me under the bed so grandpa could not whip me. I was so afraid of whippings; I got my share of them from my mother. She would have to chase me down to whip me. She got tired of chasing me. After chasing me one day, she whipped me for running from her first, and then whipped me for what I suppose to have done. I stopped running after that day, because running from her was causing me to get double whippings. I would be running and screaming. I tried to do everything right so I would not have to get them. I think she enjoyed it. After my episode with grandpa about fanning the flies from Grandma, I straighten up and paid attention to what my job was.

I liked taking care of my grandma, we were in-separable. I was the only granddaughter that she lived to know. There was one grand-son he was one year older than I. He was her oldest son's son. That uncle had eight other children but they lived quite a ways from us. I don't remember them being around very much. I was about eight years old when I remember first visiting them.

Grandpa always planted a big garden every summer. I was afraid of worms. Auntie would pick greens from the garden and sometimes my mother would be over visiting. She would help clean the greens. The greens would have little green worms on them. My mother would get such a kick out of scaring me with those worms. She would chase me all around the yard saying she had a worm to throw on me. I would be running and screaming. My grandma would yell at her to stop scaring me. She said that would cause me to have night mares. I don't know how old I was when she stopped chasing and antagonizing me with them.

One farm we moved to we met a white family, they were also leasing land. (This was called share cropping.) They had two little girls, Betsy and Jennifer; I finally had met some one to play with. We played together whenever I had the chance, mostly week-ends. We were too young to know anything about being prejudice. Evidently their parents didn't teach that to them. My grand parents certainly didn't, we became very good friends. Kids are not born prejudice. Since they were doing the same type of leasing as we were they moved a lot too.

My friend came over one day and told me they would be moving soon. I cried because that meant I no longer had anyone to play with and I would miss them. Jennifer was the oldest. They had a little stove that we girls would cook on. It burned real wood. We were always playing house and cooking on the stove. She wanted to sell it to me for five dollars. We didn't even have five dollars to spare. I really wanted that stove. I could not understand why I could not have it. I thought grown-ups always had money. Since I was losing Sue, the stove would have been something to remember them by.

My grandpa wanted to buy the stove for me he just did not have the money to spare. I forgave him. I loved my grandpa he could do no wrong. We would go walking together each evening to get the cows. He would teach me songs and tell me about Jesus. He taught me a song title, "(I KNOW IT WAS THE BLOOD, ONE DAY WHEN I WAS LOST, HE DIED UPON THE CROSS, I KNOW IT WAS THE BLOOD FOR ME".)I would look up to the sky on cloudy days and it seemed as though I could see Jesus in the clouds.

Back then we only went to church once a month because of the distance and the inconvenience. The old people would tell us kids when it was thundering and lightening we had to be quiet because they would say, God is doing his work. They even told us old wives tales that when it was raining and the sun is shining at that same time, the devil was whipping his wife. We thought it was true. I was grown when I learned the real truth about the devil.

When I was four years old, my grandma taught me a poem. Back then they were called speeches. All the kids had to learn one for the Easter Sunday program. I still remember it. oh sister, sister, come and see it's not a bird it's not a bee, oh It settles on the row, now it rises up and go" I said it at church on Easter Sunday very loud and clear with authority. The people would clap and give me a standing ovation. My grandpa was a preacher. Sometimes grandma, auntie and I would go with him to preach at various churches. We would have to ride in the wagon. They took blankets so I could sleep in back of the wagon on our way back home. Some times it would be late at night when we reached home.

Grandpa was very small in stature and had a dark complexion. My grandma was very jealous of him. Even though she was blind she was still beautiful. She had high cheek bones. My cheek bones are high like her. I could see she had been a very pretty woman in her younger days. I'm sure her handicap made her somewhat insecure. One day grandma insisted that gramps take her to a woman's house that she had accused him of having an affair she wanted to confront her about gramps. The rest of the family knew it was her imagination; but he took her there anyway just to please her. Of course the woman said she didn't know anything about any affair with her husband

We moved from that plantation and moved into a larger house on another plantation. My mother's youngest brother, Uncle Mack also still lived at home but he was hardly ever there. Uncle Mack was very outgoing. He was tall, handsome, and a ladies man. He had deep cow-licks and wore his hair waved with Murray hair wax. He did not own a car, he walked everywhere, walking and singing. My uncle love to sing. He had a voice that everyone knew. They would say, "We hear Mack coming." It's a shame he didn't pursue professional singing. My grandma worried a lot about him because of the life he lived. He loved the women and they loved him. He had lots of them. Grandma would tell him he needed to change his life and get married, because the road he was traveling was going to get him into trouble if he didn't change. Before grandma died, she had that chance to know Uncle Mack got married. He married a girl name Bea and that's when his trouble started. Getting married only escalated the problem. She was very out going and maybe a little too friendly with other men, and she was also very cute. Uncle Mack was jealous temperamental. They both did not let any grass grow under their feet. The grown-ups thought I was too young to know what was going on. I knew who liked who. I was afraid my dad would find out that his friend, Mr. Robert liked my mother. He visited us lots. They all liked to go partying and grandma was concern about their life style.

LOOSING MY GRANDMA

I was five when grandma died. I had lost my best friend. We did not have the type of funeral parlors that we have today. They would embalm the bodies and bring them back to your house. The funeral director would dress the bodies and keep them at home until time for the funeral. Before we were ready to go to the church I asked if I may see my grandma one more time. My grandpa put me up in a chair so I could see her. "I cried out; "MY grandma TOOK CARE OF ME ALL THIS TIME NOW SHE'S GONE AND LEFT ME!" Everybody in the room went to peaces. I didn't see how I was going to make it without her. To me she was all I had. I only had two years with her.

I continued to live with my grandpa and Auntie until I was seven. I loved my Auntie and she loved me too. She was my mother's baby sister. Uncle Mack and Aunt Bea lived with us too. Some times I would sleep with them. I loved her very much. I loved every body. I was just a lover. Aunt Bea spent a lot of time with me. She was young at heart. She seemed to understand how I missed my granny. Uncle Mack was my favorite Uncle, he and my mother's older brother. But Uncle Mack was around the most. He was their baby brother. The older brother Uncle Jape was married before I got to know him. I don't remember him being around. When I went back to live with my parents we visited him and his wife lots.

One night I was sleeping with my Uncle Mack and Aunt Bea. The three of us were waken and heard some one whispering and counting out eighteen formal matches on a center table beside our bed. The match box always was on the table to light the lamp incase anyone had to get up through the night. All three of us heard it. We lay very still. The next morning the eighteen matches were on the table. We could not figure out what that meant, and we never did, but in eighteen days, Uncle Mack was in trouble. We said that it was grandma trying to warn him. I guess some would call that superstitious, but we three heard the counting, and every one saw the matches on the table the next morning. Everyone else was sleeping in different rooms when it happened. They did not believe us when we told them what we heard. It was around two A.M when we heard it.

Before my sixth birthday, every summer around the same time; the Quaker people would drive pass our house with a truck full of raw furniture to sell. They made rocking chairs and swings for the kids and grown-ups. I saved my money and purchased my own rocking chair. My dad was so proud of me He told everybody that his baby was responsible enough to save her money to buy her own rocking chair. They were made from all wood. I would take it back and forth to my parent's house when I visit them. I love that chair

My mother's oldest sister Dolly was married to an older man, Uncle Frankie. He had children from his previous marriage. One of his daughters was married to Mr. Robert. She died soon after her first child was born. Rumor had it that she was poisoned. My Aunt and uncle took the baby and raised her as their own along with his children. They never had any children together. Mr. Robert never married again. He became a ladies man. He was very handsome, and had one eye. He liked hanging around with the family. I don't think my dad ever found out that he had an eye for my mother. I never heard him raising hell about that, although he raised enough hell about other things. It's hard to fool kids. I knew Mr. Robert was sweet on her. I think she liked him too, but I never saw them do anything wrong.

One Saturday evening they took me to our neighbor's house to stay while they all went to a party. Aunt Bea was always so frisky and flirty. I heard the older people talking and said, "Aunt Bea called Mr. Robert a one eyed son of a B; and he slapped her. She ran and told Uncle Mack, but she did not tell him what she had said to him. Uncle Mack never said a word. He walked fifty feet to get a double blade axe from a man's wood pile; he came back and hit Mr. Robert with the axe and split his head from ear to ear.

It was the next day when my parents arrived to pick me up and told me what happen. I heard my parents say when Mr. Robert fell; "the blood flowed like water down a gully after a BIG rain". I was so sad; I knew my Uncle was going away for a long-time. No matter what the crime; everybody served a term of five years in the penitentiary. It was not the same five years as these prisoners serve today; it was HARD–labor. I loved Mr. Robert too. He was fun to be around. Uncle Mack went to Jail; he was found guilty, and was sent to serve five–years on that Farm.

We would visit him on the farm. The prisoners all wore black and white striped clothes. He told us how they had to work the fields and that you must keep up with your group. If that guard walk through, and you were behind that line, you got beaten right there with a big black belt. This belt had a Big– hole in it. It was design to suck the flesh through the hole every time you were hit. They had Chef's, who were also prisoners; and they would prepare dinner for the guest. But we never would eat. We had heard rumors that worms were sometimes found in the greens. My dad told me when he was in that same prison; he was beaten until that little leg would swell up as big as that normal leg. People very seldom would repeat a second offense and return back there. Some times they show that prison on TV as a documentary on the History Channel. It is still in operation.

3.
Dad's Accident

I WAS STILL LIVING with grandpa and Auntie. Early one morning my mother came by to tell us that my dad had been burned very badly, and had been taken to the hospital. I was scared because I really was a Daddy's girl. I didn't know how severe he was burned. Early that morning before day break, he was fixing something out on the porch, and accidentally knocks the kerosene lamp over that he was using for light, and set himself on fire. He rolled himself off the porch onto the grass which was wet with the morning dew, the dew on the grass put out the fire. A neighbor took him to the hospital. Children could not go to Hospitals to visit back then. I had to wait until he came home. The doctors would use a technique where they talked the fire out of a burned patient. I asked my mother; how do they talk the fire out of a person. What do you mean; they talk the fire out? I was always full of questions. But she did not know the answer. That's what they did in those days, all we know is it worked. My dad soon came home. He had second degree burns.

I would go back and forth and visit with my parents. Sometimes I would stay a week or two. My dad said he would miss his little girl, and he would come and get me and my rocking chair. I took it with me if I was to be gone a while. I would stay with my parents a while and go back to my grandpa's house. It was more excitement at my grandpa's; because Auntie was lots of fun. She would make popcorn candy, peanut brittle and we would boil fresh peanuts, and play games. She thought she would never get married. She had passed the old maid age, but she seemed to be a happy person and fun to be around.

MY DAD'S COOKING

When I turned six I would visit my parents regularly. When they have verbal fights, mother would leave me and my dad to fend for our selves. They would have some hollowing; and screaming drag outs. They both were temperamental. She would pack up and leave us. I would miss her. My dad would cook corn bread and get butter milk from Miss B across the road and make us milk and corn bread. That was our morning breakfast. Then he would take me to Miss B's house. She would watch me until he came home from work at the mill. At dinner we would eat what was left over from what we had for breakfast. Some times Miss B would cook and send food over to us. She had a couple of kids too.

My Aunt Dolly and Uncle Frankie were busy raising their grand baby. When she got older I would visit often. They named her Lea. They moved in a house where my dad had once lived. He had planted a fig tree in the back yard when he lived there. When my Aunt and her family moved in the house; the tree was grown and baring big juicy figs. We would eat them until the season ended, and they were all gone. My Aunt told me that I was a baby when my daddy planted that tree. I visited her and Uncle a lots. Some times I would spend week ends with them. Lea started dipping snuff at the age of five. We would go to the fields together with Uncle Frankie and Aunt Dolly. We were too young to do much work. Those old people would make you do what you could. They would get blood from a turnip.

Lea would pick up snuff cuds that other people had spit out from their mouths and put them in her lip at age five. I would tell my aunt. Every time I told on her, we would fall out. So my Aunt said; "I'd rather buy the snuff for her than have her using what has been in other people mouths". That was too; unsanitary. She bought snuff for Lea. Aunt Dolly and Uncle Frankie raised all her step children until they were all grown up. They loved and called her mom. They loved and respected her through their life time.

Lea and I did not get along sometimes. She was light skinned; and thought she was all that. Aunt and Uncle had her spoiled. And she could do no wrong. After Aunt Bea left the scene; nobody spoiled me the way they spoiled Lea, I guess I was jealous.

Aunt Bea and Uncle Mack never got back together after he got off the prison farm. He got wild again; and met and married Aunt Bea's first Cousin and he had Children by both women. Their kids were cousins and sisters. His children and I also played together sometimes. He would bring them to visit us. I was a bed wetter, and Lea and I would sleep together. She would make fun of me. I would try to stay awake at night trying not to wet the bed, when I wake up the bed would be wet no matter what I did. I wet the bed until I became a teen.

When Lea grew up she met and married Aunt Dolly's Nephew which was my first cousin. They had many children. He was the Grandson that was one year older than I. She died in her early fifties from Lung cancer. She never stopped dipping snuff. I never saw much of them after they were married.

When I was seven I came to live with my parents permanently. We moved out east of the City on Mr. Sawyer's plantation. He was a prominent black man with a wife and four children; they owned their own plantation. My dad leased farm land from them for two years. While we work that land, in my dad's spare time he decided to build an automobile. He was very gifted; he could make and fix almost anything. His hobby was working on cars, guns, and filing saws. It took us one year to complete the automobile. I say us– because I helped. Some one gave him the frame and he bought parts, found parts, and some parts were donated. I helped by passing him his tools. I learned a lot about fixing things by helping him. He taught me the names of everything he worked with. When we finished the auto, we took it for a test drive. It was ready. From then we were never without an auto, because if it broke down he could fix it. We went from a T-Model to an A-Model car. My dad never changed from the A-Modal. He was very old fashion. He never rode on a train. He never saw any other parts of the world

The Sawyers had two daughters and two sons. The youngest son and I were sweet on each other. We were about eight. When my dad worked in the field, I was the water girl. One day when I was carrying water to my dad, the youngest son and I decided to meet under the bridge to do what we called get some. (Sex) We did not know how to stand up and do it. There was water under the bridge where we met, and was standing, so we couldn't lie down. We never got a round to trying that again. We really didn't know what we were doing, at least I didn't. He kept asking if I would give him some I said ok. I never saw his pe-we. I didn't even know what one look like.

His sister was in her twenties. When I would go to their house to visit she would have me come into her bed room. She would lie on her bed and tell me to play with her private part; she would tell me that was her and my secret. I did not to tell any one. The rest of the family would be home too. She would close the door. My mother had not told me anything about the birds and the bees yet, so I did not tell any one until now. I did not think grown ups would tell kids anything wrong. I knew it seemed wrong; but I was taught to honor my elders. She was my elder. I had no knowledge about how cruel grown-ups could be. I was to learn more about that later.

When I was growing up I had a lots of tummy aches. My mother said I had worms, and she would give me worm medicine. She said that would make the worms pass out. I thought they would be crawling out of me. I would be afraid to go to have a B M because we did not have toilets. We had to go to the woods and squat and hope no one saw us. I was afraid the worms would crawl out. Mother never explained how the medicine would work. I was so afraid of worms; I would not go when I felt the urge, so I stayed constipated. I would be on top of the hill crying trying to have a B M, but I could not. I would call out to my mother, mother- mother- I can't do- do- She would call me in and give me a laxative. My dad teased me about that until I got married. He would say mother- mother- I can't do- do- to my friends when they came around. I suffered with constipation for many years because every where we moved there were no inside facilities. They all were out houses built out a ways from the house. In the winter time it was too cold to use them. In the summer time it was too hot and I was afraid of the snakes. They like hanging around those types of places in the hot summer time. I was in my thirties when we moved to a place with inside facilities. The adjustment to my body came slow. I was so blessed not to have suffered with hemorrhoids like my mother did.

My Auntie came to live with us. She was twenty four. She had never been married, and did not have any children. She was still my favorite.

She raised me until I was seven years of age. I was so happy when she came. We would play games with the peanuts. She taught me how to play a game called; "Old Gray Horse. She would say, "Old Gray horse" I would say I'll ride, she would say, "how many miles" I had to guess how many peanuts were in her hand. If I guess which hand was holding the nuts, I would get all them. The peanuts represented how many miles. I really do like peanuts, raw, or cooked. I order them in twenty five pound increments often.

We also raised peanuts. They grow in clusters at the bottom of the vine. Harvest time is usually in October. When pulling them from the ground; we had to be careful because some times snakes would rap around the bottom of the vines. When we shook the vines, the snakes would fall off. My mother was not afraid of snakes. When she was pregnant with me; she would run catch them and kill them. I don't know how true the old saying is; that a mother can mark the child she is carrying in her womb by the things she does. If that be true, she marked me. I am so afraid of snakes I can not watch them on TV. We would boil the peanuts in salty water while they are green. That is how we made salty peanuts. We would also dry them out and bake them. My mother's favorite was raw peanuts. Cracking and eating peanuts is therapy to me.

My mom and dad had some friends; Jack and Linda, whom they would go partying with. They lived about thirty miles from us. One week end they invited my Parents to go with them to a Friday night party. I don't know why my dad didn't go. He said it was ok if mother goes with them. They picked her up on Friday evening, and brought her back home on Sunday after-noon. My dad asks my Mom why she didn't come home sooner, she said; "that she had told Linda she needed to go home before Sunday. Linda said; "Oh, Ted don't mind, you're with us". My dad's nick name was Ted.

When my Mom went to bed that Sunday night, my Dad went outside, cut a limb from a tree, came inside, held my Mom down; and beat her until she was bloody as an animal. My Auntie and I could not pull him off of her. Her clothes stuck to her wounds for weeks. Auntie and I tried to get her to go to the doctor; but she would not go. She used different herbs from plants and certain tree leaves and made salves out of the leaves, and applied them to her wounds until they were healed. My dad never told her he was sorry.

My Mom and I attended the same church as Mrs. Linda and her family. I never knew my dad to go to church. I was almost nine; Mrs. Linda asked my parents if I could participate in a church play. It was a Tom -Thumb wedding. She wanted me to be the bride, and her son Lee would be the groom. We thought that was funny. Lee was only ten. We practiced for weeks getting ready. By then we kids thought we had fallen madly in love. We were silly to think we were married, because the grown-up's teased us a long time, calling us husband and wife. We thought we were girl and boy friend. We moved again. Auntie moved with us. Lee and I thought we would never see each other again. We really had a crush on each other.

We never told any one about the beating, not even Mr. Jack and Mrs. Linda. 0We leased farm land from my dad's sister Aunt Meg and Uncle Dan. They had a large plantation. My mother named me after her. Every one called us Maggie. After I grew up I found out that Maggie, Peggy, and Margaret was the same names. I choose Margaret; I did not like Maggie, because I really did not like her that much. She was a school teacher, and that seemed to make her think she was too high and mighty. She only taught summer school. I had turned nine years old and had not started to School yet. Every where we moved, the schools were so far away; that my mom just didn't bother to send me. I attended a little summer school under Aunt Meg.

I was always getting scolded for not paying attention. If you send me to get something; by the time I reached where you sent me, I would have forgotten what you said. I was such a happy child. All I thought about was playing. I enjoyed playing jacks, Jumping rope, hop scotch, bicycle riding, and braiding anything that had three ends. When I would go with my mother to someone's house, if no one were there for me to play with, I would sit in their yard and braid the grass if it was long enough. I had the gift to be a Cosmetologist but I did not recognize it until much later in my life.

All the ladies wore nylon stockings. When the stockings became too ragged to wear, our parents would cut them into strings and wrap our hair with them that looked similar to the braids worn today. The War of 1942 needed all nylon to make powder bags and Parachutes. The

Government took away all the nylon. We could not get any more nylon hosiery. We had to wear cotton stockings, all of them were light tan. We hated them. We could not duplicate any other material for rapping the hair. Nothing else would stretch like that nylon. Rapping the hair caused it to grow healthier because it was protected from the elements and did not get too dry

4.

The Post Hole Digger

My Dad did a lot of outside work after we moved on Uncle and Aunt Maggie's farm, such as mending fences and fixing whatever was broken. One evening he sent me up to Aunt Meg's to get the post-hole digger. It was getting late and he wanted to get finished before dark. Her house was about three regular blocks from our house. When I got there I had forgotten what he sent me to get. I was forever forgetting. I only thought about playing. There were other families who lived on their land with children. We all played together. I went skipping back not a care in the world, "daddy; what did you say? He said wait just a **god dam** minute. He cursed just about every word especially if he hit his hand while working on something. My dad got that belt; he put it on my **derriere;** when he finished whipping my **derriere;** I sang; the <u>post hole digger;</u> the <u>post hole digger;</u> all the way back to her house. After that whipping, I paid attention. If I had to sing about what I was sent to get; I did whatever it took not to forget. And that also taught me how to manage my life. Being forgetful can cause one to lose your life. Every Summer I would stump my big toe; and tear my nail in Aunt Meg's yard almost every time I would go to her house. I walked with my head in the air like my Mom. Aunt Meg had her walk way laid with uneven bricks it was beautiful but hard on my feet. We kids did not wear any shoes in the summer because most of the time we did not have any to wear summer, or winter. I remember one winter some one in the family heard about a white family had boxes of shoes to give a way. Some one went and got them for us kids. Some of them were high heels but whoever could fit a pair, could have them.

Aunt Meg had two steps sons; one of them was sweet on Auntie. They got involved; she got pregnant and had a son, I baby sat him. She was more like my mother. I had lived in the house with Auntie seven of my nine years. Her baby seemed like my little brother. They did not get married. She moved on and was married several years later and had several other children. I always stayed close to auntie. She had a memory like an Elephant. She had two girls and six boys. They all seemed as my brothers and sisters. One daughter died in a fire. She and her husband burned to death in the apartment fire. We were devastated at that tragedy. Auntie raised her daughter and thank God; the baby happened to be with auntie when the fire broke out. Thank God for Grand Parents. She turned out to be a very respectable young lady. She was too young to remember her parents. The other daughter and I grew up together. She and I call each other sister even today. We keep close touch with each other.

We moved again. My father was tired of farming. He got a job at the Sawmill filing saws. That paid little more money than farming did. We moved into a big house. Linda parents, Mr. and Mrs.Coleens lived on top of the hill. Their kids would come to visit their grandparents. My little boy friend Lee would come too. We were so happy. That gave us a chance to see each other even though we had moved. We would build go-carts and drive them down the hill. There was not a spot of grass on that hill. We all looked like dust rats. I was a tom boy because there were never any girls to play with. Jack, Linda, and my parents, started going to parties together again, only this time, her sister Ms Naoma had joined them.

When they would go out to the juke joint they would take us kids and some covers. We kids would run around playing until we got sleepy. Our parents would put us down to sleep and cover us up until they were ready to go home. Ms. Naoma would get so drunk that she would not know where she was. Men would take advantage of her while she was drunk, sometimes she would be on her cycle. My mother would take her home with us to keep the men from taken advantage of her. She was so skinny and puny looking. My mother felt sorry for her and would fix her a place to sleep right in the room with my dad and her. It turned out that my dad had other ideas. (More about that later.)

My Mother's Warning

Mr. Colleens was in his eighties. My mom was twenty nine. Mr. Colleens would walk down the hill to our house to talk to my mom. She was a people person. There were no other houses near. He would walk down at least twice a week for his exercise. He and my mom would sit on the porch and talk a while. Their mother told Linda and Naoma that my mom was having an affair with their dad. These are the two sisters who were supposed to be my mother's friends. They sent one of the kids to tell my mother to come up to their mom's house. They were waiting in the bushes with an ice pick to stab her to death about their eighty year old father. He had a Hernia so large he could hardly walk. My mother said she had a funny feeling to come over her. All she could see far a split second was blood, and that her mother appeared before her. She was warned in her spirit not to go. She headed to the warning and did not go. For some reason after that, the relationship grew cold. Mother had no idea they were angry with her about their dad.

Later years they saw how foolish they had been, and told my mother about what they had planed. They found out that their mother was confused and in her first stages of dementia. My mother knew how to be your friend, without being at your house. She did not do much visiting. She taught me not to wear my welcome out. She taught me how to keep my friends close, and my enemies closer if I can tell the difference. She also taught me that beauty is not beautiful if it is not inside of you. Pneumonia and tuberculosis was the going disease in those days. My mother would talk about how not to expose my body to the cold, always dress warm, and always leave something for the man's imagination. He does not always want to see it before he get it. My mother taught me very positive things; she just neglected to tell me about the boys, and what I should not do with them. We lost any contact with those sisters. At least my mom did. Lee and I never saw each again until many years later. We were both grown.

5.

Meeting My Sister for the First Time

WE WERE LIVING IN that same house. It set a ways back off the road. I was home alone one after noon. I don't I remember where my parents had gone. It was so lonely out there. There were no houses near by. I could hear the Whooper Wills (a Bird) calling all day. That is the loneliest sound. Even today when I hear one calling; it takes me back. I was pretty good at entertaining myself. As I was playing on the porch; I saw this big long black car driving up to our house. I had not ever seen one that big before. A lady got out and asks me if daddy was at home. I'm thinking who is this calling my daddy her daddy. I said (noom) that is what we said instead of no. She asks if I knew who she was, again I said, (noom), and she said; "I'm your sister". Tell daddy I was here and I'll be back.

That following Saturday we went to town, and accidentally ran into her. People from certain areas would congregate on certain sides of town. Since we lived on the East side of the rural area, we hung out on the East side of town. What a coincidence; my sister was down Town shopping and we met up. I was so happy to know I had a sister. My parents had not told me about her. She was the sister I mention earlier that my dad had by his first wife. There were also two brothers. One brother died of Pneumonia. I heard my parents talk about him. His name was after my father. I met my other brother much later. He volunteered for the Army at age fifteen. He was so young, and still wetting the bed when he volunteered. I really loved him and my sister. That was a dream which came true.

My sister was in her early twenties. She was married to Presley. They had two children one walking and one in arms. She was a Cosmetologist; her husband a limousine driver. That was the big car driving up to our house that day. When my sister found out that I was nine years old and not in school, she was devastated. They started to work on my parents immediately.

They finally convinced my parents to let me move to town to live with them and go to school. They had a hard time convincing them to let me go, which meant I would have to leave them. They finally agreed. Not long after I left, they moved to town. My sister found a house across the street from where she lived and told my parents that the house was empty, and that she would put a hold on it if they wanted to move to town. They said they wanted the house and they moved in. The house had plenty of room, but it seemed my dad had problems with roomy houses.

After school I would do my home work, then I would baby sit for my sister while she work. She worked long hours in her home. I was not confined to baby sitting. The kids and I had fun. Presley would give us money and we would go down the street to the snow ball stand. I would put the baby in the buggy, and his little sister who was two years old, would walk and hold onto the side of the buggy. We would hang out with the other kids. My sister's mother lived out on a big plantation too. They would take me with them to visit her and her husband. I Called her Mama Bell. I remember her husband being ill and unable to take care of himself. He was a lot older than she. She nurtured him until he died. She was a great cook, and there was always plenty to eat and many deserts. She was very nice to me. I felt as if I was her granddaughter too. When her husband passed, she sold her farm and moved to Missouri. Her grand children had moved there. I would visit her while visiting my nieces and nephews. I always stayed in touch with her until she died at age ninety six. When she passed her grand children who were also my nieces and Nephews called me to let me know. I went to her funeral. She saw all her children die and leave her. She never said anything to me about my dad. She never talked about when they were together. I really never knew that much about my dad. I never knew his parents; I don't know how he got cripple or anything about his child hood. He did tell me his mother's name and that my sister had her name. He told me he completed the twelfth grade. That was a very good education for kids back then. Even this day; some never go that far, or if they do, that's as far as they will choose to go. I didn't ask her any thing about my dad. I wanted to, but I thought I'm just a kid; I better not.

On Sundays we did not do much church going. My sister would cook a big breakfast, Smothered pork chops, home made biscuits, rice, gravy, chicken and sausages. That's the way most people prepared breakfast in the South. We could taste and smell food in those days, not any more. I was growing tall, so I was a big eater. My job was to do the dishes, but I was lazy. I did not want anybody to tell me what to do, and I had a nasty attitude. My sister got tired of that attitude, so she talked to me about how ugly it made me look. She said you are a pretty girl, but your attitude makes you ugly. I changed my attitude because I did not want to be ugly. Society goes by looks. It's sad but it is true. I did not know that then, but I learned all about it later in life, and matt"10: 29 sums it all up, about what low self-esteem and beauty is all about. It goes to say, one of the psychological diseases of our modern culture is, how our consumer society mass-markets beauty, youth, and material success so that we are constantly bombarded with images of people we see as better than ourselves, and the tendency to compare ourselves with the perfect body, face, job, or intelligence of another leads us to feel inadequate. Jesus encourages us to locate the proper source of self-esteem. Our lives are of infinite worth, not because we have the looks of a model or the mind of a Nobel Prize winner, but because we are created and loved personally by the eternal God of all heaven and earth. When our self esteem is grounded, not in ourselves, but in our creator, we are free from a destructive overemphasis on self.

I was very tall for my age, I had to start school in what they call pre-primmer, now it's called kinder garden. When the higher grades would change periods, the teacher would open the door, and those kids would point and laugh at us. It was about five of us in that class. The boys in our class would harass us girls. I was skinny and had big eyes; they would call me eyes-. We girls hated them especially, when the teacher would leave the room. They would jump in our seats and feel our breast and try to kiss us. They were too old to be in that class too. What really made the difference was that we went to devotion twice a week. We were taught that God was our creator. We had the Ten Commandments on the wall in the chapel. Those Commandments taught us the rules of God and kids enjoyed being kids. They might fight, but they had respect for their elders. Parents whipped kids buts like the bible said. What happened? It is because God is being taking as secondary

My sister lived parallel across from the school and her kids went to that same school. The structure of the school was from pre-primer through twelfth grade. Our teachers taught education to the point that when I quit school at fifth grade; my children have said to me that I knew more than they were being taught in high school. The teachers would even paddle our behinds and kids were not coming back to the school with a gun to kill the teacher or class mates.

My parents lived in that house a year before moving across town. Then I had a long ways to walk to school. My mother had hemorrhoids very bad. One day she was boiling some water in a pot so she could steep the swollen hemorrhoids. She told me to bring the water from the stove, and pour it into the chamber pot; and as I removed the boiling water not paying attention, I spilled some of that hot boiling water on my foot. First it became a blister, but I continued to wear my shoes and go to school. The foot became so infected that I had to stay out of school for a few weeks. I really didn't need that. I had to catch up with the class. I was already too old to be in that class.

6.

Moving into the Ark

THE NEXT YEAR MY parents moved again into a two room Ark. As you can see my parents were the most moving people ever. The Ark was too small for our family I had no privacy. It had only a kitchen and a front room. I lived with my sister most of the time. When I would come home in the winter time I would sleep in the front room with my parents, which is where the kerosene heater was. It would only heat up the one room. One night that heater over heated and was getting ready to explode; my daddy grabbed a blanket off the bed and raped it around that heater and took it out side to cool. I always thought my daddy was not afraid of any thing or any one. Being crippling did no stop him from doing anything. The unit was so small, in the summer time I would sleep in the kitchen on a cart whenever I was there.

My dad worked as a mechanic at an Auto Shop. Two men came to the Shop and got into altercation with my dad about their Automobile. They called him names, all kind of cripple son-of-a-b s. My dad got so angry; he walked home and got his shotgun. When I found out what he was doing, I ran behind him begging him not to go back to prison. Thank God when he got back to the shop the men were gone. My mother was at work when it happened. I told her what had happen and how frighten I was; she just shook her head and never made a comment.

My class-mate lived across the street and she was an only child too, and was being raised by her grand mother. Their house sat on a hill. We would go up town and get card board boxes and open them up so we could run jump on them and slide down the hill in her yard. A bunch of us girls would also play husband and wife. I was always playing as the wife. For some reason in the back of my mind; being a wife was intriguing to me. She and I fell out one day because she stole my piece of glass that I had found. I had an idea about painting a picture on it. It was such a beautiful piece of glass. I wanted to become a painter. I showed it to her and shared with her my idea; she took the glass without my permission and would not give it back. I called her a thief; and had a hard time forgiving her.

As we got older; around eleven, we girls would participate in a lot of school plays. My teacher would find a place for me in every school play. My mother got tired of buying different outfits for me to participate. The school had scheduled a play coming up soon, and my teacher selected me again to have apart in it. I needed a white dress. I did not have one. My mother said "no not this time". Another class-mate said; "she had three white dresses, and I could borrow one of them". My dad did not allow me to borrow anything. I beg my mother to go talk to, her mother to borrow the dress. I really wanted to be in the play, so we went over my dad's head and we borrowed the dress. The night of the play as we stood on the steps lined up to perform; the girl told all the kids that were in line; "the dress I had on was her dress". I was so embarrassed; I almost forgot my role in the play. I didn't ask for the dress. She offered to let me use it, we were play mates.

At school she and her other friends laughed and bullied me about that dress. They even threatened to fight me. I was always a loner, and afraid of fights. One day she came over to my house to play, the dress was brought up again. I was tired of hearing about it. I got so angry I beat her butt well, and we became the best of friends and remained so until she died. The only other fight I was ever in was about me speaking up in behalf of a new girl in our class, who was very homely looking and the kids were poking fun at her. After school, one of the girls who were involved in poking fun told her brother that I got smart with her, the whole family of four jumped on me. All I could do was hold my head to keep the licks from my face. It really wasn't a fight; because I never passed a lick. If you are not that person who fights a lot, you most likely will not be successful conquering a fight of four people.

I don't know where C.W and H.R were that day. Those were my boy friends. C.W didn't live in the Quarter where we lived; he lived in West-Ward; about five more blocks past our Quarter. H.R lived in the same Quarter as I did. They would walk me home from school every day. They were always arguing about who was going to walk me home from school and carry my books. It finally ended into a fight between the two; and C W. threw a rock and broke H.R's front tooth.

My dad would tell them about my bed wetting. He thought if he could embarrass me enough that would help me to stop. I would be too Shame to face them. But I still could not control my bed wetting. I was a very sound sleeper. My Dad would yell, and curse me up out of bed for school every morning. I would have to bathe every morning before I go to school to keep from smelling like urine. When the school room got warm there were others we knew had that same problem because we could smell them. H.R did not get his tooth fixed until he went into the Army. We all grew up and went our own way. C.W and H.R remained there in our home town. H.R passed away. The last time I visited my home town my cousin and I were shopping, and she introduced me to C.W's sister. I never knew he had a sister. I told her the story about her brother being my boy friend when we were kids, and how he and H.R fighting over me. She laughed and thought that was so funny.

I never thought I would get married and have a house full of children. I dreamed of being a movie star, making plenty of money, and taking care of my parents. I met another girl who was the only girl in her family. She lived on the next street up from the Quarter. She had an older brother but he was hardly ever around. She was one of the girls that would play the marriage games with us. We would go up town and get huge empty cardboard boxes and cut windows in them and make houses. She and I would talk about how we wish we were related.

Sometimes our mothers would visit each other, the conversation came up about people they knew, where they were raised, and naming names of relatives they both knew; and found out we were cousins. We were so happy to be related to each other. We became inseparable. My dad had made a bicycle for me. I was the only girl with a bike in the neighborhood. The Police Department had started a law that all bicycles had to be registered; and that we must ride our bikes on the same side as the traffic. When I took my bike into the police station to check my serial number, they could not find one for my bike. I told them that my dad had made it. He found pieces here and there and put it together. It had no fenders, but it was well put together. The police looked at each other and laughed and sent me on.

Later on into that summer my cousin came by my house one Saturday evening riding a red bicycle. She told my mother that it was her cousin's bicycle. She asks me if I would go home with her and tell her mother that the bike belong to my cousin. I went and told her mother that lie because I had no idea it was stolen. Stealing was not a word that we were accustomed to. People left their doors open, and bicycles in the yard, or whatever you wanted to leave outside.

That Sunday we went riding on our bikes, as we entered the intersection, a White man came running out of a restaurant at the corner saying "that was his daughter's bike that was stolen the night before". "He called the Police". We ran home and ran behind the Ark in the Quarter where we lived. We saw the police driving down our street slowly. We knew they were looking for us, so we came out from behind the building. When they saw us they stopped and told us to get into the police car. I was so scared; as we got in the car my parents were coming to the door and they saw the police car pulling off with us in the back seat. They did not know what was going on. The police was riding us around questioning us. I really didn't know anything because I didn't know she had stolen the bike. She didn't tell me where she got it from; I just told her mother what she asked me to say. That was a lesson learned, don't just say what someone tell you to say with out asking questions. We children back then got our butts whipped about lying.

The Police took us to my cousin's house to talk to her mother because she did not know anything about what's going on. As we was in route "I was telling them that I had my own bike; and reminded them about the time I brought it into the station to be registered, and how they was so astound that my daddy made my bike. They said, "We remember that bicycle". When we got to her house and the Police told her mother "what they had us for", her mother said to me; "Maggie you told me that was your cousin's bicycle; why did you tell me that lie?" I looked her in the eye and said; I did not tell you that. She was determined to get to the truth of the matter. The Police decided to let our parents handle the situation. They left her house, and dropped me off at my house. She and her mother came to our house to straighten out the mess. "She told my parents what I had told her about the Bike". "I stuck to the lie, because I knew I was going to get it one way or the other. But I knew I had to tell the truth because I really did love her mother. I always wanted people to love me. I did not want her to dislike me because I had deceived her, so I told the truth. I don't know what her mother did to her. When my parents finished whipping my butt, from that day I respected my elders and I never told them another lie. That whipping caused me to be turned off to people who lie; I hate it, it's not necessary to lie. There is a difference in a person who practices lying; from a person who tell <u>a lie. Even </u>if the lie is to save a life; you must repent, because God hates any kinds of liars. He said a liar can not tarry in His sight.

We remain friends until I left town. We didn't see much of each other after that. I really did not know what happen to her and her family. I found out that her lifestyle had become very wild and she died at a young age. When I got married and left Mississippi, I lost contact with all the friends I grew up with.

7.

The Two Room Ark

BACK TO THE ARK; for those who may not know what an ark is, they were something like projects. This one only had two rooms per unit, and each unit was joined together. You did not have to get on the ground to go next door. A young single Lady lived next door. After we got to know her, she would ask my mom if I could spend the night with her sometimes. Spending nights with people back then was a common thing. We had never heard anything about being gay or Molestation. We used the word gay as meaning happy. Even though it was going on big time back then, we did not know anything about it, or heard anyone talking about it. As I have said before; our parents never told us anything

Essie was never disrespectful toward me, and she always treated me as her little sister. She did not have any family there. Sometimes when I would spend the night; she would sneak her boyfriend in the back door, and when they thought I was sleeping, they would ease into bed and began kissing and hugging, then he would climb on top of her. I would play sleep and they never knew I was awake. I always slept in bed with her; I never mention to her what I had heard. I thought it was just something that grown ups do; my parents did that too, when I slept in the same room with them; I could hear them making that same noise like they were.

I was grown before I heard the word Molestation. If some one touched me in a private place on my body, I knew it was wrong; and

30

I did not want to be around that person alone I did not know it to be a crime; and that people went to jail for it; or that it was called abuse. It mostly happens from relatives, or old men sitting around the house visiting; or some one who is very close to you; and your parents never believe you when you tell. Sometimes it could be women. Men aren't the only ones who molest kids.

One summer my mother left my dad and took me with her to the country. We moved in with her brother and his wife. We would help them with their crops. When the fall of the year came and it was time for school to start I would have to stay to help with their harvest. I would be late starting school I would have to catch up with the class. I was a Smart kid but school was not important to my parents; or any parents we knew. They considered work more important than school.

Most of the parents that lived in that geographical area would make their kids work in the fields until the crops were all finished, and then they might; allow them to go to school. I was reading at the age of four and five on my own without any teaching. As my parents and I would drive through town and I were seated in the back seat, I would be reading the signs and talking to my dad about things they did not know I knew about. I told my dad that I did not like people with two faces. He said "what do you know about two face people"? "Who told you about such word"? I explained to them; People who pretend to be your friends, but don't like you, and they say bad things about you behind your back, and grin in your face. My parents were shocked; they said in a low voice "where'd she learn all this"?

My dad started to teach me the Lord's prayers. I could not learn that prayer for the life of me. He would listen while I try to recite them. If I miss a word he would yell at me. I realized it was the fear of his yelling; I said to him, "I have never seen you say your prayers why are you yelling at me? My dad stopped having me recite them before him, and I learned them very quickly.

I matured very fast. When I was eleven my cycle had started and I wore a size C bra. My dad started to rub his beard across my face and feel my breast. I really loved my dad; but I knew something was wrong with that picture. I would be squirming trying to get away. He would be holding me too tight to get loose from him. As I have said "we kids knew nothing about incest or molestation. One week end we spent the night with Uncle Mack and his new wife. My parents and I slept in the same bed. My mother was in the middle; and my dad was reaching over her trying to feel me. I fell out of the bed trying to get away from him which woke my mom up. She asks me "What are you doing falling out of bed?" I said I don't know. The next morning I told her what had happen. She said;

"Do not to tell your uncle because they were both hot heads". She did not want any trouble. As I began to grow up and started maturing; she accused me of being the culprit. She said "I acted fast around my dad." I never was a fast kid. I was always too shy. I did not talk much as I got older. I was always afraid I might get a whipping, because I got lots of them.

When auntie got married, she and her husband would come over to visit. He would set me on his lap and thrust his body up and down. I would jump up off his lap. I knew that was out of order. One day I went over to their house, her husband was home too, I whispered and told my auntie what he had been doing to me, she locked the doors, we beat his butt until he broke out that door. Her children helped. They did not why, but they were just helping their mother. We always had lots of relatives visiting our house. Grandpa's cousin Dottie and her son Dank would come by often. He was a little retarded. He was so-- funny; the way he talked and looked, but we loved him and enjoyed him. Cousin Dottie was so short. She had no legs. She used two very short walking canes about two feet tall, to take her wherever she wanted to go. She could get up in a chair and get into the kitchen cabinets and cook what ever she wanted to cook. She was really a good cook. In the fall of one year; the flood waters rose from so much rain; Dank drowned. We were so sad, and missed him. He could say the funniest things.

My dad had another sister name Mary. she and her husband had three sons. We visited them often. They lived by a lake. They would catch turtles and frogs clean them and cook them. She was such a good cook. I really did love visiting her. She had a kind sweet spirit and was nothing like his sister Meg. We would spend many week ends with them. My dad believed in visiting his family. She died long before my dad, at a very young age. She fell from a horse. She never recovered from the fall. Two of her sons still live in different States, but we never see each other.

ARMY BASE

When the Military Base first opened up right out side the town, it brought lots of jobs to the town. There were also lots of the women that were falling hard for those Solders. The Health department were busing loads of woman to a near by town to clinics to get treated for syphilis. There were stabbings, cutting, and the crime was running rapid. One solder got stab in the unit next to us. People were coming from every where looking for places to sleep so they could work. There were no motels or hotels for blacks.

People were renting sleeping quarters to whoever needed a place so they could work. It also brought income for the people who were renting them places to sleep. My parents rented four young ladies the front room. The four of them slept across the bed; just so they could work and make some money. The jobs lasted about six weeks. My parents need the money too.

When The Jobs all ended, and the Ladies were ready to go back home, one of the young ladies ask my parents "if I may go home with her." "They said; "yes I could go". I was happy to get the chance to go some place for the summer. I was tired of working the fields each and every summer.

That turned out to be the worst summer I ever had. The field would have been a pleasure; compared to that summer. She lived in something like Cul-de-sac. The houses were close together and everybody had kids. She had two sisters about my age. The kids did not like me, It might have been because I was from what they call the city. I was blamed for everything they did, and was scolded for things the kids said I did. My parents really didn't know them that well, to send me off with Her. We had only been acquainted for six weeks. I don't know if she knew I had a problem wetting the bed. That was a devastating experience. I did not know those people. They would look at me as if they were wondering; why did she bring her down here.

When it was time for me to go home; I was a happy child. But I was sad that my friend Essie had moved. One of my mother's first cousin Nelly and her family moved into that unit. She had one daughter name Julia, and her mother who we called Any, lived with them. She also had a son name Bubbie. He was in the military. After they moved in, we met Bubbie later when he came home on leave.

Not long after they moved in; my mother left my dad again. This time I stayed with him so I could go to school. Usually when she would leave she would take me out of school to go with her. I could not understand why they fought and separated so much. She had moved to Tennessee. It was good timing when Cousin Nelly moved in, because I needed a female adult around, but I spent a lot of time at my sisters, she lived across town. I would tell myself; when I grow up and get married I will not be separating and going back and forth. I was going to stay in the relationship as long as I could; and if I ever had to leave; I would only leave twice. If it did not work after that second time of leaving, it would be over. It did not make any sense the way they carried on. We can say; what we have not done; but we can never "say what we will not do. I turned out a lot like my mother in relationships. We have a tendency to do what our parents do.

Her daughter and I hit it off right away. We were always at each others unit. One evening we were all gathered over in our unit; and a man knocked on the door to leave a gun for my Dad to fix for him. The man said; "the gun was not loaded."

We were all sitting around the dresser laughing and talking. I kept picking up the gun snapping the trigger. Nobody had electric lights. We all used kerosene lamps for lights. Our lamp was sitting on the dresser where we were sitting. One last time I picked up that gun and began snapping the trigger. The gun went off and every one was quiet as a mouse. The powder from the gun when it fired put the lamp out. Julia was sitting at the end of the dresser, I was in the middle, and her mother was sitting at the other end. I was so scared that someone was dead. It was piercing dark. Nobody was saying a word for a second.

We finally found a match and lit the lamp. Every body was ok. Her mother kept telling me that it was not my fault. I was afraid that my dad was going to give me a terrible whipping for playing with the gun. But the worst scenario; I could have killed somebody. When my dad came home and was told what had happen he was angry with the man not me. When he came back to pick up the gun my dad cursed him out!

Julia and I would spend nights with each other sometimes. We both were lonely for a sister. She would help out with her grand mother. Like us they had two beds in the front room. When ever I would spend the night she and I would sleep together and her mother and grandma would sleep together. When Julia came down with the mumps I tried to catch them. She would sleep with her mouth open; I would get in her face so she could breathe on me. I never got them. We would talk ourselves to sleep. When Bubbie came home on leave from the Army, he slept on a cot in the kitchen.

He got up early one morning and sat in a chair on my side of the bed and puts his hand under my cover and was touching my private part His mother saw what he was doing and she only says to him in a mild tone; "boy you know better". I expected her to run him out of the house. I was his cousin; and I was just a kid. I was too young to know what his intentions were. I knew he was touching me in an in forbidden area and his mother was so mild about it. I was thirty when I found out what a clitoris was, and then I understood what his intentions were.

My daddy always believed that we had sex. Her Son would hang around all day trying to get me to let him have sex with me. I always heard my Mother say "you do not have sex with family. (I put it mild) about the way she said it. I spent the night With Julia after he had returned back to the base. I wet her bed. I was so embarrassed; I told my dad that my bladder was hurting. He took me to a doctor way out in the country to examine me because he thought I had had sex. Daddy had also found a condom that Bubbie had given me. I didn't know what it was, so I threw it in the garbage, and my Dad found it. That really aroused his suspicion about us. I was always afraid that my Dad would come in at night and touch me, but he never touched, or rubbed his beard on me again. He stayed out a lot at night. I would be home alone most of the time. He came home one morning while I was at one of the ladies units, who lived in back of us, getting my hair braided. He gave me a whipping because I went without his permission. So many guys were always in the Quarter; I guess he feared something would happen to me because the women were selling their bodies to the soldiers for money. Cousin Nelly had given me permission to go.

8.

Sailor on the train

AT THE SCHOOL BREAK my cousin, Julia, her mother and I went to visit my mother In Tenn. She was living with this cousin Nellie's sister. We took the Train there. I had never been on a train. Trains were popular then. Most people traveled by train. They had just built this one called the City of New-Orleans; and it was swinging. When we heard that it would make its first run through our town; I think every one in that town went down to the train station to see the new train. It was red and black in color, trimmed in silver. I was so excited to get a chance to ride this exclusive train. I was extremely happy to see my mother. I really wanted to stay with her but she was not stable enough to keep me there. Bubbie and his girlfriend were also visiting there. They had no respect for us kids. They were all over the floor smooching. I got the impression he was trying to show me that because I didn't let him have sex with me he could make me jealous. I was still a kid but I did feel a little remorse because I could not tell him off. My parents never knew what he had tried to do to me. Cousin Nelly knew. That probably would have been the time to tell. I never saw him again.

On the way back from our trip there were lots of Sailors on the train. They were all over the place. One of them asks if he may sit with me. I said it was ok. He asks my name and wanted to know if he could call on me. I said ok because I thought he was kidding. I was just a skinny tall kid with big eyes. He gave me a genuine leather wallet. I did not know it was genuine leather, until my dad saw it and asks where I got such expensive genuine wallet from. I told him a Sailor on the train had given it to me; he took it.

A few weeks later my mother came home. Her cousin she was living with convinced her that I was at the age I needed her to be at home with me. Why would some one have to tell her that? She was so use to running off when she and my dad argued. I would think to myself; if she did not leave him for good; when he whipped her that night with that big stick, then why leave for something so much less; and keep coming back. That was when she should have left and never came back.

One Sunday after noon there was a knock on the door. It was the Sailor and he asks my parents if he may call on me. They said "nooo! She is just a kid". He came back a couple of times. The last time he came, he asked if he may marry me. My Parents said; "nooo!" Then he asked if he may give me a gold tooth to remember him. They said; "nooo!" I really wanted a gold tooth. I did not think I was too young for that. It seems that every one who went north and came back south had some gold on their teeth. I said when I get grown; I'm going up North and get some gold put on my teeth. But when I did move north the fad had changed. The Sailor came around a few more times. He saw that my parents were not changing their minds, so he finally gave up on me. I heard he had married some girl not too far away from where we lived. One of my school mates saw him later and he told her, "I sure wanted to marry that girl. I never saw him again. I was eleven and soon to be twelve. All I wanted to do was play and ride my bike.

Julia and I would go to the movies every Saturday. Movie tickets were only ten cents until the age of twelve, and then they cost twenty five cents. I had to fight with the ticket agent every week. Because he did not want to believe I was still eleven. I was glad when I turned twelve so he would get off my case. After Julia and I got out of the movie one Saturday evening, the sun was still shining. There was a Carnival up town a few blocks from the theater. A young man asked Julia and I if we wanted to go with him to the Carnival. We said yes, we went with him. The first ride was the fairest wheel. It only holds two, so he took me up first. When the ride ended it was dark, and Julia had gone home. She told my parents where I was and that I was with a man. The young man walked me home. I told him that I was going to get a whipping. He asks, "If I wanted him to go in with me". I said oh no; that would have been worse because I was only a kid and he was at least twenty years old. When I got to the back door I could hear my dad saying; I was going to get it. I was afraid to go in; and afraid to stay outside too long, because that would make them think I was still with the man. Julia was not as old as I was; and she was fat and had a sweet eye. So she felt as if he took me up because he thought I was the cutest. She left me. If it had been the other way a round, I would have stayed with her, and we both would get the punishment. I did get the whipping. If she had stayed; I probably would not have got the whipping. I ask her why she left me; she said she was scared. She had to tell the truth when my parents asks where I was. I think it was a little jealousy.

CUTTING MY TOE

When school would end for the summer, a bunch of us kids would catch the trucks which were gathering people to go work in their fields Monday through Friday. We had to be ready to get on the truck at four a:m or we would get left. That is how we kids would purchase our school clothes. Being kids, we would add a little play time; but if the Bosses catch us goofing off; we could get fired, and we would have to wait around until the end of the day when the trucks leave to take everybody home. The sun is hotter when you were not working. Cotton choppers; were paid by the day. And cotton pickers got paid by the pounds. Some times my mother would catch the trucks at cotton picking time, which was in the fall of the year. She would pick three hundred to three hundred fifty pounds of cotton. She has picked up to four hundred pounds. At summer time, the weeds would grow and smother the cotton plants, so we were hired to cut the weeds from around the cotton plants so they could grow. At cotton picking time, we would pick the cotton, put it in the sacks, and weigh the cotton, then dump it into the trucks. They would give our sacks back so we could fill them again. When the cotton truck was full; they would take the cotton to the Gin to transform it into fabric and whatever is made from cotton. We would continue to fill those sacks until time to quit at five o'clock that evening.

When it is cotton chopping time, we always had our lunch at noon; the Bosses would sharpen our tools at that time, so we could have them sharp enough to cut that tough Bermuda grass. It is such a tough grass to cut, that the tools must be very sharp. It was quite a few of us kids working in the fields. One of my friends; and I were playing tag, hitting each other and take off running, we would go chasing after each other.

After the tools were sharpened; and we had returned back to work. The Bosses had left the field and we start playing. We were tagging and chasing each other. She hit me and I went to chase after her, she dropped her hoe and ran, and I stepped on the corner of it, and cut my toe to the white meat. I was afraid to tell my parents because the grown-ups had told us to stop playing. We were going to chase each other one more time and stop; because if you did not obey your elders they would whip you and tell your parents; and you would get another whipping. All your elders were like your parents when the parents were not present.

I continued to wear my shoes to field, the weather was hot. By a day or two; my toe had set up inflammation. My parents did not believe in going to the Doctors. My Mom made up her salves; and applied it to my toe and I suffered through that pain until it finally healed it self. I missed the rest of that summer going to the fields. Cotton chopping is usually over by the end of August.

When my foot healed enough I got a job baby sitting a little white kid without my dad's permission. My mom said it was ok. She did day work for a family of three. I would be so happy when she worked their house parties, because she would bring home the food that was left over. That food would taste so good. Their daughter always fought with her weight. She was eighteen and love to sleep late. My mom would have to beg her to get out of bed so she could clean her room. I was happy to baby sit the little boy, because It made me feel like I was walking in my mom's foot steps. But when my dad found out; he was furious and made me stop. He said I was not responsible enough to take care of any kids; and that he was not going to have me hanging from a tree because something happen to that kid. I really did not want to stop. The child, and the parents liked me and the kid cried. But father knows best; because hanging, and lynching was still happening back then, and there was no limit on age or gender.

My mother was a hard worker. I never knew of any time when she was not working. She never bought herself any clothes. She always wanted a couple suits. Some one came through taking orders for hand made suits. Merchants were always coming through selling something. My mom saved up enough money and purchased herself two beautiful suits. One of them was a beautiful green and gray. The top half of the jacket was green, the bottom was gray, and the skirt was all gray. The other one was all black. When my mother took them to the cleaners and they were ready for pick up, she sent me to get them. We only lived four short blocks from the cleaners. She did not expect any problems because she had used that cleaner for years, and they knew her well. I think it was the only cleaners in town. When I got home, there was only one suit in the bag. Some one had taken my mom's gray suit. She was so— hurt. When she went back to confront them they told her; "I must had dropped it from the bag on the way home, because they put it into the bag." There was nothing my mom could do about it. It was a child's word against theirs. I know I did not drop the suit. I was walking with the bag folded across my arms in front of me.

My mom met a man whom she started seeing periodically. She would take me with her sometimes when she would meet with him some place. They would just walk up and down the street and talk. I never saw them do anything else. It was ok with me. She and my dad were always arguing about something. I said, at least she has some one she can talk to. My mother would never let me go to any of my friend's house to play. It was ok if they come over if she was in a good mood. If she wasn't; she would call me into the house pretending she had something for me to do. I asked her one day if I may go over to a friend's house to play ball. She said no; I said, you won't ever let me go nowhere; she said; "well; you ain't going". I said to my self, I'll fix you. I was so angry with her. When my dad came home I told him about the male friend she had. I was getting back at her because she wouldn't let me go play ball.

That caused the biggest mess. My parents fought verbally about that for weeks. My dad cursed and raved for ever. My mom never knew how my dad found out. I was sick about it. I thought they would never stop fighting. I prayed that they would stop talking about it. I said; Lord if you help me through this I will never do this again; this has taught me a lesson. I knew better than to do that. They didn't need anything to get them started at each other. My mom left my dad. He finally went and got her. I will not ever get into anybody's business again; I will not grow up being a trouble maker. That really taught me a great lesson about doing things to get even. That kind of stuff can get some one killed. As a young child it taught me to see and not see if it's going to cause trouble. As I grew up I realized that I was being prepared to be a listener to people problems and keep them to my self. It was teaching me not to be a gossipier. That incident took me a long time to get over. I truly asked Gods forgiveness.

9.

My Uncle Bill lost his I sight

My dad had one living brother Uncle Bill. He and his wife had sixteen children. After they had their fourteenth child; he began to loose his eye sight. My dad said, his Doctor had warned him that if he did not stop making babies, he was going to loose his eye sight. He was making them too fast. He did loose his eye sight. They had two more babies after being warned. His wife told my mother that even after he lost his sight, he would chase her around the bed before the baby was six weeks old. I don't know if that was the reason he lost it.. He never saw his last two children. He learned how to get around where ever He wanted to go. One of his children became his guide. He and my dad were very close. We visited them a lot. I was told at one of our family reunions my dad had another brother. I never knew about him. My dad never mentioned him. Uncle Bill's oldest daughter Flo and I were one year apart. We would spend a few weeks during the summer, at our Aunt and Uncle's Plantation to help them out. They were getting up in age. Aunt Meg was always so slow.

Before Flo started joining me at there home, I would go to stay with them and help in the fields. I could chop a row and a half before Aunt Meg got one row done. One day I ask; if I may do the laundry for her; she said; "you don't know how to wash clothes". We did not have washing machines back then. We heated water and used a wash board, and plenty muscle. She finally agreed. I did such a good job, and it did not take me all day. After that, she worked me too hard. I should

42

have never asked. I did all the hard work. When Flo came she got all the goodies. She favored her because she was from such a large family. I under stood that' because I really did love Flo. She and I also lived together at my sister's.

My cycle started at age eleven, when I reached the age of twelve, it had stopped. Every day I would get so ill. I told my aunt, when the sun would reach its hottest part of the day around noon in that hot field; I would have to go to the shade and lay down. Aunt Meg asks me if I was pregnant. I did not know what she meant; nobody had told me if your cycle stop, that could mean you are pregnant. Uncle had leased a spot of their land to a Doctor and his family. He was an herb Doctor and could mix up herbs for almost anything. My aunt asked him if he could mix up something to re-start my cycle. He said he could. He made up some medicine and brought it the next day. In a few days it worked. He asked me to meet him at an old abandon house that was on my Aunts property. He said he wanted to examine me. I knew he liked young girls. His wife was very young. They had two young boys. We all worked that whole summer together. I stayed away from him. I did not trust that reasoning.

We learned some other things about him. He was also a psychic. Every evening when we all finish work, they would travel back to town where they lived, which was about thirty five miles from us. One evening we were all sitting at the dinner table talking about the Doctor, nothing bad just general conversation. When they arrived that next morning, he told uncle and Aunt Meg everything they had said about them. I would pray every day that he would not ever catch me alone. Why the old abandon house? God answered my prayers. I did not trust being alone with him. They only leased land that one year.

As a child I had knots on both my eye lids. (Stars) we did many things to get rid of them. "Some one told my mother to get a box of hankies; take me to the flak of the road; have me throw the hankie over my shoulder, keep walking, don't look back, and the knots would go away. They were so ugly on my eyes. One other thing we tried was tweezing all of my eye lashes out. That was so painful. Aunt Meg would set me between her legs and tweeze out a few each night. That did not work either, and then my eyes lids were bald. I was without eye lashes and still had the knots. My eyes looked even worse, because now they are big, bald, and the knots are more noticeable.

Aunt Meg and uncle had a large house. Both sons were gone now. I had my own room when I would visit them. I was sleeping late one morning; I heard something making a noise on the wall. The walls were wall papered. I open my eyes there was a long snake crawling on the wall. I screamed so loud; my aunt came running to see what was wrong; she said; "oh" "it's not harmful; it's just a king snake." "It is looking for mice." That was the end of my staying with them.

When I returned home my dad decided to do something about those knots on my eyes. I was growing up now; and they looked so ugly. He took some formal matches, trimmed them sharp as a tooth pick, sterilized a pocket knife, sat me between his legs, he cut the skin under the lid and circle around that knot with the sharp tooth pick and squeezed it. The core popped out. He did both eyes and they never come back. My big pretty eyes could be seen for the very first time. But the eye lashes never grew back. Only dawns grew in. They had been so thick before the tweezing. Now; I can't even wear the false ones because I have no lashes to attach them to.

When my dad was married to his first wife, He was working on a project; a small peace of steel flew up and wedged into his eyeball. He went to three eye doctors. Each one told him; "that eye would have to be removed". He would not say a word; he just gets up and leaves. After his third visit to three Doctors, all said the same thing. My dad went home and asked his wife to hold the lamp light. He took a pair of tweezers and got that peace of steel out of his eye. He had twenty, twenty vision until death. So what could be so hard about removing two little knots from his little girl's eyes? He did it, they never came back.

THE WRONG GUN

My father had fixed two guns for two different Gentlemen. He told my Mom which gun to give to each customer when they come to pick them up. She gave the wrong gun to the wrong man. I knew that would be something to start their usual fight. I told my mom about the Doctor that I had met at my uncle's Farm, and that we should go to see if he can help us. She agreed to go. We went to see him and told him our situation. He took out his Crystal Ball and showed us that there were two men. One waited out side across the ditch that separated our house from the street, while the other man came in to pay for his gun. We had to cross a plank walk to come into our yard. It was a concrete ditch that the water ran through when it rain to keep the little yard from flooding. There was always running water in it. He showed us the one guy crossing the walk to the yard and into the house. We saw him come out with the gun; and he and the other guy got into their Auto and drove off. He showed us what Highway to take to get there, and that the house he lived in set off the road.

When dad came home we told him about the mistake and we told him that we knew where the man lived. We did not tell him how we had found out. He had to drive us to pick it up because my mom didn't drive. That was one time I wished she did drive, but he was ok about that. We knew the area because we use to live near there. That was where we lived when my Sister come driving up in that big car. We went to the customer's house and exchanged the guns. That did diminish that-fight but the fighting between the two of them never got any better. Mother was a spic and span house keeper. She did not allow any one to set on her bed. That bed spread and pillows had to be just right. You better not move her curtains to look out of the window. They fought a lot about her moving his tools, not physical, but words don't heal. As I said we only had two rooms. He had no place to keep them except in the house, and that was no place for them. We could not get him to find larger living quarters, so that I may have my own room, and that he could have a place to keep his tools. We really had no place to sit. I had never seen a couch until I visited my sister. I thought they were rich. I guess the rent must have been next to nothing, because my dad was tight. He would buy only rubber boots. When he would take them off at night; we had to leave the room. Jews own that four block Quarter. The only time we saw the land-lord was when it was rent time dad would take it to their house, which was on the main street, right across the yard from the Quarter. There were never any empty units. It was called; Jew Quarter. People seem to like living there.

10.

I Accepted Jesus Christ.

I KNEW MY MOM really" wanted to get away from all the abuse; and leave Dad for good. I begin to pray for a husband. At age twelve; mother took me to a revival that was being held at our church. A bunch of us kids and older people sat on the mourner's bench. That is what they did at revivals. We would sit there every night for two weeks until the revival was over. By then I had heard enough about Jesus to make a quality decision about my salvation. I accepted Christ into my life and was baptized in a lake. I really understood what I was doing. I read my bible every day. I did not under stand a lot of what I was reading. I would ask God to help me under stand. And he would do that. So I believed if I prayed for a husband; God would answer me. In the south one could marry young if some one of age would sign for the license. Mother had left my dad and me again. While she was gone; I met my husband. His name was Jahari C. Jr. They called him J.C. Dad said that stood for Jesus Christ because of my actions when he drive up and blew the horn. When Mother returned, and found out I had a boy friend; I think she was happy. She would let me go to the movies with him, but not my Dad. I could follow him around all day asking him if I may go to the movie with Jahari, and he would never answer me. I knew I better not go if he did not answer me. When dad heard Jahari blow the horn he would say; Jesus Christ is here, because I would be so excited. Jahari always came and knocked on our door and spoke to my parents. When I would go to the movie with him dad would not be at home.

46

Jahari had a cousin who lived in the third door down in the ark. She would let him and me come in to her apartment and sit around on her bed. Of course there was no other place to sit. There was no room in those units for a couch. Her daughter and I became friends. Her name was the same nick name as mine. When they moved into the Quarter, she and I both was an only child; and our mothers called us by the same nick name. Koot was our nick names. Because of that; we figured that we should always be friends. I don't know why her mother called her Koot. My mom said she called me koot; because I was so cute when I was a baby. We thought that was such a coincident. She and I went to the fields together on those work trucks and made our money to purchase school clothes.

One summer she and I purchased some fabric and had two skirts made the same. They had ruffles all around the tail, and all the way up to the waist band. They were called Penny Fold skirt because of the ruffles. Then we had a play suit made the same. We would go over on the next street in front of the unit, To the Café and put money in the juke box and dance. The Jitterbug was the popular dance. The unit were built to go around three blocks. Every unit was facing a street, South, West, and East. That's why it was called a Quarter.

Koot and I became so close that one did not go to the toilet without the other. The quarter where we lived had toilets outside, but they were flushable toilets. Each section facing a street had it's own outside toilets. Koot lived in the third door down from me, which made the toilet closer to her door. When she would go, she would knock on my door; and I would stand outside the toilet door and talk to her, and she would do the same for me. I really wanted a little sister. Before I met her I would look in the catalogs and beg my mother to order me a little sister from the catalog. I could see they were only little white kids, I did not know they were not real people. I thought she could order one my color. She never told me any difference. She always told me she got me out of a tree stump. I thought she really did find me there. Koot and I had been in the same class together since we met. We didn't want to separate from each other, when she retained the fifth grade; I needed to go to summer school in order to go to the sixth grade. I refused to go. We were hoping we could remain in the same room; but we got separated any way. We were in different rooms even though I retained the fifth grade so we could stay together. I no longer wanted to go to School. She was the only friend I had. I only stayed in School five more months.

Jahari and I had known each other about three months; before he began to mention sex to me. Every time he asks; I would tell him I was on my cycle. I was afraid because I had no idea what that was all about. Finally he got hip to that lie. He said to me; you are going to bleed to death. Mom still had not told me anything about sex. I thought by now if there was anything to tell me; now was the time. She was allowing me to date; but she was still telling me that Stump lie. She never told me about my cycle. I was at school while she was away; and I had an accident. My cycle started at school while sitting in my seat. It was so warm that I did not know until I got up out of my seat to read. I did not wear any panties that day. I did not have any clean. I was still in a child's mind doing childish things. I did not think the night before I needed to wash a pair of under ware. All I thought about was playing. Mother was gone again. Daddy was not there. I had no directions. The person seated behind me alerted the teacher. I was so embarrassed. I did not know what was happening. My teacher took me out of the room and fixed me up. I was too ashamed to go back into the room; because all the students and those same boys who were always teasing us girls were also in the room. They never said anything. They were real gentlemen. Sister never told me anything either. She was like my mama. Parents just did not talk to their boys and girls back then. I was still staying with my sister most of the time. Why didn't she talk to me? She had two girls; the youngest one was born after I was married. Her older daughter that I baby sat and I slept together in a twin bed. I was still wetting the bed. No matter what anybody said I could not stop.

11.
I Lost My Virginity.

I KNEW IN MY heart; that as soon as I leave the nest, my mother was leaving too. Jahari and I went to the movie one Saturday evening. I was really into the movie. I really liked those romantic movies, I was dumb enough to think that's the way life was, and would be. Instead of Jahari watching the movie; he kept watching me, so I said to him lets go; because I didn't want to loose him. I was willing to do what he asks. No one had told me you do not have to give up your body to hold on to some one if he really loves you. I thought sex was love. I thought if I didn't he would be gone back to Illinois.

I was in love with him because he was my first boy friend. He was so neat. His clothes fit him like he was poured into them. It was real love; because I felt that same feeling twelve years after we were married. We left the movie and drove out on a country road and parked the car; I climbed into the back seat, that's where I lost my virginity. Parents please talk to your sons and daughters; don't leave anything out. Tell them the truth! I was only thirteen. I knew nothing about what I was getting myself into. A few weeks later; one evening Jahari came to visit; my parents left us alone while they went two doors down to visit a neighbor. He talked me into what he called a quickie. That quickie later had a name; he was live and well.

I would be turning fourteen in one month. I had been living back with my parents for a while. My cycle had stopped again. I thought it was the same problem as before, so I said nothing. About six weeks later, one day I was running and playing, I felt like something was shaking in my stomach. It would hurt when I run. I love running and playing and riding my bike. I would ride down the hill in the middle if the streets with no hands on the handle bars. Sometimes I was guiding the bike with my feet on the handle bars. I was a real tom boy.

I knew a girl who lived on the corner of my street who had had a baby. He was about one year old. One day I asked her what she did to get her baby, and how she felt when she got pregnant. We were not friends, she was much older, but she would play with us some times. That next day I rode my bike over to my sister's house. I told her that I had missed my period. She was going to take me that following morning to that same herbal Doctor I had met at Aunt Meg's, to get an abortion. My sister had never heard of him. I told her about him and where I met him, and that he did do abortions. He only lived about four blocks from my sister.

The girl that I had asked about her pregnancy; had gone and told my mother that she think I was pregnant; and that same night my mom and dad came over to my sister's house. We didn't lie about what we had planed to do. They both were so disappointed and hurt. I was hurt too, so was my sister. My mom called me every name she could think of; and believe me; she could call you plenty of them. When my dad had heard enough name calling, he stepped in; and told my Mom; that's enough; that if she had been around to teach me, and be a mother to me, it probably could have been avoided. I did not know that was where babies came from. I thought they came out the tree stump like she told me. I thought if I did it that one time with Jahari that will shut him up, and that he would not ask me any more. When he asks the second time; I just did not want to ever say no to him. Being afraid to say no because you think you may loose some one; is bad business. If you loose them because you say no; you didn't have them in the first place. I never dreamed I was getting a baby. All my friends turned their backs on me. I had no one.

Koot my best friend turned away. A young girl stood alone if she got pregnant and were not married. Every body talked about you, even at church they whispered. You had no place to turn. I was blessed to have Jahari to turn to. But I was too young. I missed out on life. He was there for me. His cousin told him she had heard that I was pregnant and that he was too young to get married. She told him to go back up North. She was the one who allowed us to come into her Unit and sit on her bed. I thank God; we both love each other. Thank God he is the Father of all eight of them.

Dad didn't seem to like Jahari. I did not know why but I found out later, that he already knew him. Jahari lived across the road from Ms.Naoma. He had seen him visiting her. She was the lady that my mom had taken home with her and my dad many nights to make sure that she was safe when ever she was too drunk to take care of herself. Jahari never told me until years later. I never told my Mom. That affair had been going on all that time. About five years. I was eight when my Mom would do those favors for her.

Jahari had been living up north with his elder brother and his wife. I called her my sis. His Brother was not a Pastor yet. I met Jahari a few months after he came back home to live with his parents. My sister and her family lived in an apartment complex cross town. I was spending the week-end with them. His cousin thought if she warns him about the pregnancy; he could run back to Illinois and not face his responsibility. But instead some one told Jahari where I was, and he came to that complex looking for me. He did not know which apartment my sister lived in. There were about five rows of unites in the complex. She and her family lived at the end apartment of the first row on the main street which he was driving on and blowing his horn.

THE PROPOSAL

Jahari and his brother U drove down the street blowing the horn. I knew that horn where ever I heard it. I went running out the door. By then they were a ways down the street. He saw me through the rear view mirror and backed up, he got out of the car and said to me; "I heard that something is wrong with you" (meaning pregnant) I said yes, he asked, "do you want to get married? I said yes, we set the date for two weeks. His grandpa said; "he would sign for us to get married". His sister and I were in the same class, but I did not know she was his sister at that time. I had befriended her because class mates can be so rude. If you don't look the way society thinks you should look.

She was a new student from the country and some of the kids would make fun of her. I was always the one who reached out to others. I guess the fight before did not stop me from reaching out trying to speak up for others. I being an only child, therefore I had to learn to be creative, and to entertain myself. I had a vivid imagination. That caused me to want to see other people look their best. I would give her pointers on how to improve her looks. When I found out that Jahari was her brother; we both were delighted that we were friends. He was seeing another girl at the time; who lived down the road from his parents. He asked his sister which one of us girls he should marry. She told him I was her choice I liked her too.

12.

Having to leave home

MOTHER SAID; "I HAD to go because I was a disgrace to her and my dad". I told her we were getting married in two weeks. But she had heard that his family owned a large Plantation and were called big shots, and that they had lots of money. Mother would remind me every day; that big shot family is not going to let their son marry a poor gal like you. But I believed in Jahari because he had driven around looking for me. He could have run back to Illinois as he had been advised to do.

Mr. Joe and Ms, Mien once lived in one of the units of the Ark. They had moved into a house across town into the West Ward of the City. She would tell me that I was such a sweet girl. When they heard my mother had put me out; they both said I could come and stay with them, since my wedding date was set for two weeks. I got married in a red dress at the court-house. It poured down rain all that day. It rained so hard we could hardly see where we were going. The only ones at the wedding were Jahari, his grandpa, the Judge, and I.

We moved in with Jahari's parents. Their names were Rev. Jahari and Helen. I called them Father J. and Mama H. I was beginning to show to the point that I could not fit into my clothes. The only clothes I had was the few I took with me to Ms. I Mien's house. My mother would not give me the rest of my clothes. I still had my rocking chair. She would not give it to me. I wanted to pass it down to my children. It was still solid as when I bought it. I don't know what happened to it. I had to wear whatever I could find. I met a Lady who lived down the road in one of the houses on the plantation that my in-laws owned. She was a seamstress. She made me a couple of maternity dresses and did not charge me anything.

Jahari's family had a big house and a large family. They were raising their two grand daughters along with their own children. Everybody lived at home, except the grand kid's mother and their elder son Louie. After the serving his time in the Army, he and his wife settled in Illinois. They had one son. Jahari's baby brother was my little friend. He was only nine and was a little handicapped. He was such a sweet kid. He would call me-Sis Mag; and follow me around talking to me and making sure I needed nothing. By the time he grew up and got married. We had moved away. I met his wife and most of his children. He has a beautiful family of daughters and sons.

OUR FIRST FIGHT

At school, one of my class mates was so hilarious. He kept everybody laughing. He could say the funniest things. If some one was talking fast, or out talking him; he would say … (stop running your mouth like a clapper bell in a goose's ass). Every time he said it we would all crack up. I thought it was hilarious enough to say it to Jahari. One evening we were all at the dinner table and he was on my case about something. Just kidding; I said to him; what my class-mate had said that made us all laugh. I thought we all would have a big laugh too. Jahari slapped me so hard I saw stars. I said take me home to my mama. He made me pack my few clothes; but while I was packing; I had a change of heart. I really didn't want to go back there. I told him I did not want to go back home, but he made me go any-way. I guess I embarrassed him before his family. I was still a kid full of fun, I was only fourteen; I thought it was funny, but when I got to my parents house that wasn't funny. My dad asked; what's the matter? Jahari said I'm bringing her home. My dad said; "don't bring her here". "Take her back; that's your wife now". My mom said, "Wait a minute; you don't know what happen. Leave her alone".

Jahari left me there. I was so empty and hurt. I thought; could it be all over so soon. I stayed there with my parents two weeks. My dad was on my case the whole time. It seemed he hated me because I was pregnant before marriage. He threatened to hit me on my head with a milk bottle one day. I wrote Jahari a letter and said if you love me; please come and get me; if you don't; I will know by your response. But he came that following Saturday and took me back home. I was so happy because I wanted to be with him. Being with him could not be any worse than what I was going through back home. Everybody was happy to have me back. Even the two grand kids, they were very young three and four and were unaware of what was happening. We were all one big family; except my father-in-law. He started in on me right from the beginning. He raised hell all day every day.

We had washed clothes early one Saturday, and they were still hanging on the line until dark. We had forgotten about them. Jahari's brother had come home and parked his auto right across the porch entrance. His sister and I thought about the clothes were still on the line. On our way out to get them; we saw a lady standing at the car with a pretty long white dress on. We both saw her at the same time. We almost knocked each other down getting back in the house. We told Mama Helen what we had seen. We described the lady to her, and she told us it was her mother. She had been dead for years. We needed the clothes from the line to get ready for church the next morning. The guys had to get them for us. It was not uncommon to hear about spirits back then. My dad could tell stories about them that would make the hair rise on your neck.

I like to day dream. I would look in the catalogs and wish for furniture to put in my house when we move from the in-laws. I always dreamed of a house of my own with nice comfortable furniture in it. I took the order blank from the back of the book and filled it out. I wrote down how many cattle and assets we had on the application. My sisters-in- laws found the application. I had forgotten all about it, because I was just dreaming. They all threatened to jump on me. They said; you don't have any assets here. I was so scared that all of them were going to jump me. Fighting intimidated me. I can count the times that I have been angry enough to fight. If I ever fight it is because I have lost control. I only remember that happening three times in my life, more about those times later.

My mother-in-law and I were like mother and daughter. She taught me how to cook, and how not to lie around too much. She said that would not be good for me or the baby. I would need to have plenty of exercise so that I could have an easier delivery. My mother didn't have the patience to teach me how to cook when I was growing up. She would only try teaching me when my friends would come over to play. I wanted to be outside with my friends. She would say, come in here and watch me cook. If I was moving like I did not want to come in; she would slap me on my head. One evening we were all out playing, she called me in to watch her cook. I was moving too slowly, the tub was hanging on the wall near the table, she hit me so hard; my head hit the tub. My daddy yells and said to her; quit hitting that gal on her head! She won't have a <u>god- dam</u> -bit of sense, you will have knocked it all out. My mom had a habit; of hitting me on my head. I said to myself when I have children; I will never slap them, call them out of their names, and I will always tell them the truth about life. I will teach them how to be productive human beings. I will ask God for wisdom to be a good mother. I believed with all my heart that He would teach me what to teach them.

13.
My Father-In-Law's Yelling

MY FATHER-IN-LAW AND I did not hit it off. He would find something every day to yell at me about. He would ride his horse behind me as we walk down the road from the field. He would go to bed yelling, and get up yelling. No one would ever come to my rescue; not even my husband. The baby was delivered by a mid wife. We were still living with Jahari's parents. The baby was a little boy; he was seven pounds and six ounces. While I was in labor I kept asking for water melon between the pains. Father J went to the field and got the water melon for me. When I found out it was he who had gone to get it; I was shocked. Mama Helen named the baby. I found out later the person she named him after was a thug–. He was a hobo and got into lots of trouble. He even got his leg cut off jumping from trains. So we stop calling him by that name, and my mother started calling him her little pet name as he got older. Names have a great affect on your life. Mama H took great care of me while I was recuperation. She said a mother could not eat mustard greens after delivering a baby. She said they would kill cows if they got into a garden with mustard greens in it after they had given birth. We had a garden full of all kinds of greens. She did not trust any one else to pick my greens from the garden. Only she would pick the ones I was to eat. She would clean and cook mine separately. I breast fed, and because of her great care, and seeing that I eat on time. I had so much milk I could hardly keep from over-flowing. I really did love Mama H, I felt like they were all the family I had and I still do.

MY PARENTS NEVER CAME

Dad and mother never came to see the baby; their only grandson. We lived in the days when sugar was rationing. People received stamps to purchase it. According to the size of the family determined how many stamps we were allowed. Dad did not want to give up my potion of the stamps. He and my father-in law had a few words about them. He finally did give them to us. He still never came to see the baby. He was walking when I got the chance to take him to see them.

The baby was about eight months old; and I wet the bed one night. I was so embarrassed. I had the covers thrown back on the bed so it could dry. We had our own bed room. But every body was from room to room. Only a big hall separated the rooms. Father J came walking through, he looked at the bed and said; "that don't look like a baby wet the bed with that big of a spot" nobody said a word. Jahari knew the truth; but said nothing. I was so glad father J had noting to start on me about that morning, ESPECIALLY that! I talked my husband into asking his father if we may move into one of the houses on the Plantation. I thought I could not take his yelling any more. I thought if we moved I would be free from him. He agreed that we could move in. In order for us to live in one of the homesteads; we would have to lease some land and plant cotton and corn. We agreed and leased the land. Father J furnish the money to purchase the grain for the crops; and when it was harvest time; we were suppose to pay the money back; and half of the harvest.. Each house had two bedrooms and a kitchen. We were only able to get a stove, and a table, for our kitchen, a dresser and a bed, in our room, and only a bed in the other room. The stove was wood burning. If the wood is not fed into it continually, the heat would not be consistent to cook the food. The houses set miles apart from each other. The plantation had three homesteads for rent on the land. Jahari's brother and wife live in one of them. They were all leased out.

Some one must tend the crops while they are growing. The grass must be cut around the corn and the cotton so the weeds do not smoother out the crops. I had to be the one to do that. My husband took a job after he had planted the fields at a near by plant where he had to carry logs on his back called Cross Tires. That was very– hard work. When I worked in the fields with my aunt and uncle; and also catching those trucks and working in those fields after school every summer; I learned a lot about working and taking care of the fields. I did the same things we did there, which was cut the grass from the plants.

I still had not learned how to bake home made biscuits. I would rise early in the morning with Jahari and cook breakfast and try to make biscuits. I would make his lunch with those biscuits. He said he would go off by himself to eat his lunch; because he was ashamed for any one to see his white biscuits. They should have been nice and brown. I just could not make them brown; but I kept practing until I became a pretty good cook.

I had to take the baby to the field with me. It was hard to watch him and work the fields. I would leave him at one end of the row while I chop the grass from a row. I would run back and forth to check on him. Each row could be as long as a half mile. I was warned that snakes can smell the milk on the baby; and go down its throat trying to get the milk. I worked in fear each day afraid that could happen to my baby. There were times that we could not drink milk from one of the cows, because she was being attacked by a snake. It would bite her tits; and cause them to bleed. When we milk the cow, all we could get was blood. Some how the men folk found out that was what was happening. They had to pen her up and give her special attention until her milk cleared up.

I did not get away from my father-in-law. He would get on his horse and go to every field until he found me. He had leased three different fields to us to harvest. He would not know which one I was working in each day, so he would ride until he found me and start up a conversation in order to find something to yell at me about. He got his kicks from fussing at me about whatever he could think of. I would never talk back. I guess that made him even angrier. I first met one of his brother's, at a church gathering. He shook my hand and scratched me in the palm of my hand. That is how men ask for sex in those days. That caused me to wonder why my father-in-law was on my case all the time for no reason.

At the end of that harvest year we had nothing coming. Unknowing to me; my husband had borrowed more than what we had coming back. As a matter of fact we ended up owning father J. Jahari had partied and drunk up our entire profit. He and his brother would go into town every Saturday; and party sometimes until Sunday evening.

I was devastated; because I still didn't have any clothes. That's what I was working so hard for. The few clothes I had, had come from the lady my mother worked for. Her daughter wore a size twenty. Mother would take her hand-me -downs and try to make them fit me sewing them by hand. She did not have a sewing machine, and was not a seamstress. I did not want those clothes any more. They did not fit any way. I wore a size seven before the baby, after that I was two sizes larger. I just knew; I was going to buy some new clothes. I was working hard mainly to buy myself some clothes which I needed badly.

CUTTING DOWN A TREE

On Saturdays when Jahari and his brother U would go to town; his brother would leave his wife with me. She was expecting her first child. If she had gone into labor we would not have known what to do; because we lived miles from any one. Sometimes they would not leave any wood for the fire. Her husband knew she was due to have the baby anytime. She was not in any shape to help me gather wood. It would get cold in the evenings. I decided to go out and cut down a tree and drag it to the house and cut it up for fire wood. Not knowing that green pine is not going to start a fire; nor is it going to burn for wood. I was also a few weeks pregnant with our second child.

I did not accomplish making the fire; but what I did accomplish was a trip to the Doctor a few days later. I had pulled my body out of place. I could not walk because of the excruciation pain. My father- in-law said; "I was faking, and that nothing was wrong with me". He said; "I was just lazy, and wanted attention, and that city children were not taught anything". "All city parents did; was feed their children and allow them to just grow up". He said; "that was all I did; I just grew up" he said; "my Parents had taught me nothing". He was right; it was a lot of things I did not know about life. I was too young. My parents did teach me to respect my elders; or I would have cursed him up one side and down the other from the very beginning; but I never did.

The Doctor was a very good Afro American Physician. He gave me a prescription that worked in a few days. He was the only black physician we had in that little town. He was well respected by all races.

Our baby started to walk at nine months old. He was such an active child. He kept me busy. I had no money to buy diapers for him. I had to tear rags to make diapers. It's hard to wash fecal stains from rags. Rags are too hard to clean because of the type of fabric. That's why diapers are made of a soft fabric, most of the time I had no soap. Water was scarce. I was afraid to go to the well, because our well was through the woods down a hill. I was afraid to go through those woods, because of foxes. They would attack pregnant women. Some other animals will attract pregnant woman too; but snakes were my greatest fear. I would sing very loud hoping to scare off any animals while carrying water. Jahari didn't carry much water. He thought that was my Job.

Mama H and I were going fishing one after noon, and had the baby in a little wagon. I was pulling the wagon and we were just walking and talking. I looked back just in time to see him with a hand full of worms getting ready to put them in his mouth. I screamed and knocked them from his hands. Our front porch was four or five feet from the ground. I would anchor a chair across the door to keep him from getting to the porch. When I would go to check on him; he would be on the ground eating dirt.

My mom came to visit us while we were still living there. Father J never came around while she was there. They were two of a kind and would have been a match for each other. Jahari and I were ashamed to make love while she was visiting us; because our bed made too much noise. I guess that was because she was never open with me about life. We would go out into the field behind our house and lie on the ground between the cotton rows in the field. We would have our love time; then go back to our bed. Thank God; it was summer time.

14.
Jahari leaves us

THAT NEXT YEAR WE moved to town. We moved in with my sister and her family temporally. Their house had only three bed rooms and there were six members of her family. There were three of us. We slept on the couch until I got tired. I knew my sister was tired too. My husband would not look for us a place to move. I went out and found us an up stairs apartment right around the corner from my sisters. The apartment sat over a garage. It was a cozy little place. Shortly after we moved into the apartment Jahari started to fight me. I was in my fourth month of the pregnancy. I would be sixteen that next year.

My brother had just gotten out of the Army. He and Jahari had gotten pretty tight. He had not found work yet. I don't know if he was even looking. Jahari and I had tickets to go see a celebrity at the foot ball stadium. He took my ticket and gave it to my brother. They said "I did not need to go." I was not going to be out done. I went to my daddy and got money for another ticket and taxi fair. I went to the show anyway. I paid at the door. I ran into Jahari and my brother. They were surprised to see me. I was pretty head strong. You did not dare me to do anything. Head strong may not have been such a good thing in certain situations. I guess that was what broke us up.

One evening my sister and I went to the movie. Jahari was never home for me to tell him anything. When he found out I days later that I had been to the movie without asking; "he asks me did I go to the movie." I said I did; and he slapped me around; and packed his clothes and moved out. He moved in with his grandpa; the same one who signed for us to get married. He left me and the baby, and another one in the making. I figured he would soon cool off and come home. The fight was so immature. Weeks passed no Jahari. I went up town one Saturday hoping to see him. I saw his father instead. It was a very–hot day. I did not have any shoes to put on the baby's feet. The concrete was so hot to his little feet. I was trying to carry him; but he was too heavy. Being pregnant; I could not carry him too far. I ask his father J if he would buy the baby some shoes. He said to me; "let your man buy him some shoes" "I ain't buying him nothing". I was so hurt! I didn't have a man, only his son; and he had left us.

My mother had finally left my dad for good; and had moved back to Memphis and was living with Cousin Nelly who had lived next door to us at the Ark. My sister had decided that she did not want to help me any more. I guess she was tired of our insecurities; plus she was having some issues of her own.

I met a guy. He said he wanted to help me because he felt sorry for me and my son. He said he would take care of us. I knew he really wanted more than just to help us. Even at that age I knew; no one helps for nothing. He would be looking for something in return. I loved my husband and was hoping he would come home. I was not about to let any other man into my life. Jahari never came back. We got so hungry and things got so bad; I decided to take the guy up on his offer. I could no longer pay the rent. I dealt with him a while because I really–did not want to contact my mother. I finally had to write her and explained what had happened. Right away she sent me a ticket; and we went to live with her and Cousin Nelly. She and her family had moved from the Ark some years before. Her son Bubbie had rented a house for her in Memphis and moved them there.

Mother was the only one in the house working. Cousin Nelly had to take care of her senior mother; who was now senile. Her Daughter was not yet working. There were six of us living in a three room house. Her Son was still over seas. We were struggling. If it had not been for the Lord, the Manager of the store; and my mother's Friend; I really don't know what we would have done. The store was facing the other street, and the back of the store was connected to our house. I think the Manager was the landlord. He would give us the vegetables when they weren't fresh enough to sell. Some times I would only get the pot liquor from the greens; but that's where the nutrients are, so I didn't complain. Watermelon was my favorite fruit. Mr. Friend treated me like a daughter. He would buy me melons every week. He would help my mother out financially. God was there all the time. He never leaves us. He puts people in your path to help when you think there is no hope.

One day I went to the back yard to throw something in the garbage. As I was walking from the yard, the truck was just pulling in to pick up the garbage. One of the guys on the truck asks me my name; and said he would like to call on me. I laughed and thought to myself; who want to talk to a pregnant woman. He came back that same evening. We became very good friends and he bought me more watermelons than I could eat. My little Son, love to slip off and go two houses down the side walk. Mother was calling him Pinny. I would switch those little bow legs down that side walk all the way back to our house many times a day. His legs were so bow; I thought they would never grow straight. The right leg almost touched the ground. They did grow straight as he grew. Slipping off was his amusement even after he grew up. I think I switched him too much. It made him tough and rebellious. Another Cousin had a Son. He and my Son were two of a kind. Her Son was older than mine. He pushed my Penny down the steps; he hit the corner of the step; and cut a big gash in his head right above his eye. I had no money to take him to the hospital. He was bleeding badly. Some one next door got some soot from the chimney, and put it on the cut and stopped the bleeding. The scar healed clean.

MY DOCTOR'S VISITS

Mr. Friend took me to his family Doctor for my pre-natal care. For some reason I was afraid to go to the Doctor's office alone. I didn't trust myself riding the bus. I was afraid I would miss getting off at the right place. I was a person that housed a lot of fear. I had never been on a City bus before. That side of town was very rough back then. The Doctor's office was on a Street which was on the news every day. At first I had to go once a month. Mr. Friend did not have a car, so once a month he would go with me on the bus. Pretty soon it was every two weeks. He never missed a trip. He worked nights. So he was free during the day. The Doctor was a little flirty every visit. On one visit, "he asked me to become his Lady; and that could be the last baby I would have". "He said; "he would tie my tubes and send me back to school, not wanting for anything". But I was still in love with my husband. Nothing or anybody could change that.

When it was time for the baby to be born, we called the Doctor. He was one who made house calls. He and his Nurse came to the house to deliver the baby, but his Nurse knew that the Doctor had been flirting with me when I would come into the office. I guess she got jealous. When they arrived, the Nurse was very mean to me while I was in labor. The Doctor had to reprimand her. It was so obvious; how she was yelling, spanking, and pushing me around. The delivery was very hard but I got what I wanted. The baby was the little girl, that's what I had prayed for.

Mr. Friend paid for everything. We were so grateful, because we did not have any insurance or money. When I returned back to the Doctor for my last check-up, I told him that I was getting back with my husband. He said; you will end up with a house full of kids and no future". He said, "I want to send you to school." "You are a very bright young lady, and I would like to show you off." I was too much in love with Jahari to hear anything he was saying. That could have been to my regret anyway. He was much older, plus he was a flirt. I never saw him again.

Jahari and I had been writing each other before the baby was born. When the baby was one week old; he stopped to see us on his way back to Illinois to look for work. The baby was a pretty little girl I even potty trained her as a new born how not to wet her diaper. I named her after my mother. I would remove her diaper and hold her over the chamber; and whisper ppppp; and she knew what that mint. We used chambers because the toilets were connected to the back porch, just a toilet, no bath tub. But at least they were flushable.

Jahari spent the night, and we talked all night. We reconciled; and he went on to Illinois to look for work. He said he would send for us; when he fined work. Mother and I were not getting along. I felt as if I would rather be back with my In-laws, than my own mother. She would get up set about her life and take it out on me. She would live in the past a lot. She would call me names, and invite me to kiss her rear. She would pull her dress up and tell me to kiss her rear and lick it to the red part. This went on too often. I walked on cotton trying not to upset her. You never knew what was going to set her off.

Jahari and I were writing each other. I asked him to ask his father if we may come back and live with them while he looks for work in Illinois. We were hoping he might find work soon. He wrote and asked his father if we may come to stay and when he found work he would pay him for our staying.

He consented; so the three of us went back to my In-laws. After a few days; father J started in on me again. It seems there was no peace any where. I began to wonder why I was on this earth. What did I do to deserve all the abuse? I wrote Jahari and asked him to come back home job or no job. I can't take this any more. At least though—all father J did; was yelled and fuss about nothing; he wasn't telling me to kiss anything like my mother was saying to me, so I really could tune him out sometimes; but I was tired of it all.

A few weeks later Jahari came home; we were trying to figure out what we were going to do. We knew we could not stay with his parents.

We began to talk about how much my mother loved him. He was that son she never had. We decided to write and ask her for the money so we could come back to Memphis, and Jahari could look for work there. She said she would send us the money. It was taking her so long to send the money; I wrote her again and told her that father J said, "That our bill was still accumulation, and that we already owed over two hundred dollars". Unknowing to me, mother wrote a letter to father J and told him off. She could really talk about you if you ever upset her. The mail box was down by the side of the road. Father J went by the mail box on their way to town. When he returned he was so angry at me, he was steaming. My Mother felt like that was ridiculous for him to be charging us. I had no idea she was going to write him a letter. Mother knew he was a Preacher; and People called him; Rev. J. My husband was named after him. This is what she Wrote him saying "**Dear J; with *your old* gray ass ; God told you to go plow; and you thought He said; go preach".** I don't know what else she wrote in the letter. I never saw it. That made him so- angry and he blamed me. I tried to explain how my mother was. He did not want to hear anything I had to say.

That night Mama H did not feel well. I went cross the hall and knocked on their bed room door, and asked her if she wanted me to cook breakfast for her in the morning. She never got a chance to answer. Father J yells to the top of his lungs **"NOOOO! I don't want you to cook me no breakfast"**. "He said" **"get out of my house" "don't you ever put your foot in my house as long as I live" and when I die; don't you look on my dead body"**. The next morning, Jahari got his cousin with his truck to take us to my father's house. I had one of those huge ten trunks that someone had given to us. We put our little belongings in it and headed to my father's unit. He was still living in that two room Ark. We spent the night with him which was a Saturday night. He did not have enough room for us to stay. My dad spent the night some place else so we could use his twin bed. Some how the four of us manage to sleep in it. He had narrowed down to a twin bed: because he had filled the rest of the house with tools and iron. We did not have any idea what we were going to do about a place to stay. The next morning I had a strong feeling that my mom had sent the money. I ask Jahari to walk to the Western Union which was just a few blocks away to check; the money was there! We got the train that same day and went to Memphis. We moved in with my cousin Ritha and Brit. They were the Parents to the son who pushed my son down the steps; while Jahari looked for work; it was a job keeping those two boys out of mischief. They were two of a kind. After a few months; nothing was opening up for Jahari. He would call his brother periodically to see if anything had open up back in Illinois. Soon his brother told him they were hiring at the Yard where he worked. He got Jahari an application; and he went back to Illinois and got the job.

When we moved in with Ritha and her family; I was pregnant again. She asks, "Are you having another baby?" I was too embarrassed to say yes. She introduced me to some tablets to abort the Baby. I tried it; and I could not hear for hours. I tried several things nothing worked. I knew that was wrong to do. I had read in the bible that abortion is murder; but because she was older; and she only had two children I valued her opinion over God's word. Mother would say to me; you having all them nappy headed youngons. Some old people called them youngons; instead of young ones. I felt defeated. I felt that I was the bad guy. My husband also made me feel as if the children were only mine. I stayed behind while he went back to Illinois to get the job. Our plans were: I would have the baby while still in Memphis; and then join him In Illinois. We had not discussed who was going to pay for the delivery; or even who was going to do the delivery. I had not been under a doctor's care yet.

15.
Moving to Illinois

JAHARI STARTED WORK AND had made two pay checks. It was only two months away from my due date. Jahari had talk to his X-Sister-in-Law which was his Brother U's first wife. We called her Big Sis. She was re-married and lived in a fairly large house. She talked him into having me come on up, and that we could move in with them; and that way I would be already there when the baby comes. The weather was getting cold. That is what we did. The kids and I got the train and went to Illinois. I was excited. It was at night when we arrived. They picked us up at the train station. We had to travel about thirty five miles from the station to where she lived. I got up the next morning I was very disappointed. We were in the Country. We had to carry water. Go out doors to the toilet! I thought; we have left the City to come up North to the Country. I really had some wrong ideas about the North. I got there time enough to find a Doctor who would check me out and deliver the baby. After two months, in October when it was time to go to the hospital I was frightened; I had not ever been to a Hospital; not even to visit. That was such a long labor. That baby did not want to come into this world. Jahari and Big-Sis took me too soon. The Nurses poking was worse than the labor pains. They would put those gloves on and go up to see how much I was dilating. I thought I would pass out. I finally had the Baby. It was a boy. We named him Jebez. He was the smallest of all the babies, He was so dark completed, and I was ashamed of him. When I breast fed him I would stay in the bedroom so no one would see him. I believe it was because I tried to abort him, but God wanted him here. Jeremiah 1:5 said; I knew you before I formed you in your mother's womb. Before you were born I set you apart and appointed you as my spokesman to the world. We have no right to try to alter God's plan. I breast fed all my babies. I got smart and started staying home until it was almost time for the baby to come before going to the hospital. As Jebez grew older; he became very tall, still dark, but handsome. His skin was smooth as silk.

16.
Mother's Brake down.

WHEN THE BABY WAS two weeks old I received a call that my mother had had a brake down. She was in a grocery store and started hollowing and screaming. It took four men to hold her down and get her into a straight jacket and get her into the Ambulance. They said I need to come see about her. As I was making preparation to go to her; I received another call to hold off; she was better and was home at her apartment. She was alone; Mr. Friend had died. He was a married man. It was like he had two wives. Rumors had it that his wife knew about my mother.

We lived with Big-Sis and family about a year, it was a little crowded. She had two girls and two boys, plus she was a little bossy and always yelling and cursing. She would curse her Husband so much; she swore that she saw his dead wife come in the room where she was taking a nap and hover over her. That stopped a lot of that cursing him. He was a lot older than her; but he was very handsome and flirty. He did not look his age. I had to skate on thin ice around him. It did not matter to him that I was his wife's friend. I'd just put him in his place and keep smiling.

Jahari found another Family who had a larger living space. In those days people would rent one of their bed rooms; and everybody shared the kitchen, and the living room. We moved in with them. Her name was Lo. I found out after living there a while, that She was not a tidy house keeper. I really took over cleaning the whole house except their bed room. She was married but was soon separated shortly after we

71

moved in. They had five children, three were teenagers and two were small. She would leave the two small ones with me a lot. The teens were at school. I didn't mind because they were no trouble. And they really liked me being around. Their mother was gone a lots. She was very attractive. We all got along fine. She was very nice and made me feel like the house was open to me. I would clean it as if it was mine own. After all I did live there. My mother taught me how to be clean, and how to get along with people.

THE AFFAIR

One day her two small children and my three were home with me. My Baby was only a few months old. I fed him, and gave the other kids their lunch and put every body down for their naps, and I decided to clean the stove.

Being a country girl I did not know anything about gas stoves. I first cleaned all the eyes. Then I decided to clean the oven. I turned the oven off and cleaned it. I had the stove shining. When I turned the oven back on I did not light it right away. When I finally struck the match to light it; fire flew out into my face and burned off my eyebrows and my few eye lashes. I was blessed that I didn't swallow that flame.

We lived there one year. After we moved I found out that Jahari and Lo was having an affair. Another couple had moved into our room. I met them and I would visit them regularly. Their names were Ms. Thel and Mr. Hern. Ms. Thel was really obese; like four hundred pounds. She liked for me to come over and talk to her. She was always in and out of the Hospital. She would beg us to sneak food to her while she was hospitalized. We could not do that. She loved to eat. She was obsessed with eating.

A few months after we moved, it was a Saturday night my husband was getting ready to go out; which is what he did every night. Since this was the week-end and my mother was with us; I ask him if I could go with him. He replied; "you don't need to go". I ask; why not, mother will keep the kids. I thought; I'll just go over and see if Lo would go out with me. I wasn't bold enough to go to a club alone. Mr. Hern had been trying to talk to my Mother; but she was not interested in him. I met him on his way to our house as I was on my way to go to see if Lo would go out to the club with me. I asked him if she was home. He said; "yes" I went over to her house. My Jahari had already left home. Lo and I were standing at the bottom of her stairs talking. Her children were making so much noise up stairs; we could not hear each other. She kept yelling for them to quite it down; so she finally went up stairs to quite the children.

While she was up stairs the phone ring; since I just moved out of her house; and I'm thinking we are friends; I mean; If you live in the house with someone a year; you feel pretty close; so I answered the phone. It was my husband on the other end. He had said a few words before he realized it was me on the phone. He had just left me at home. When he recognized my voice he hung up quickly. When she came down stairs she did not ask who it was; I waited for her to ask. I said to her; it was Jahari; she looked as if I said: your mother just died. They were planning to hook up. She was waiting for that call. I went back home very hurt. I did not tell mother what had happen. I never mention it to him either. She never treated me as if she thought I knew. As the years passed; we would run into each other; she would act as if she was so- happy to see me. I really would be happy to see her.

Before we moved from her house I was pregnant with my fourth child. Jahari beat me up while she was home. It started with him hitting me on my head with a ball. I kept saying stop, I have a head ache. He kept throwing the ball hitting my head. We ended up fighting. His Brother U had come by to get him so they could go some place together. U stops the fight and they left. After I found out about the affair; I thought that was to empress Lo to make her think she was the one he loved. He would often start an altercation when he wanted to get out.

The building we moved to was a little more private, but we still had to share the kitchen with an elder lady. Jahari took my Mother back to Mississippi. When he returned the lady had moved in. She moved in a few days after we did. She was such a sweet person. We hit it off and she became my baby sitter. When mother dreamed about Cat Fish; she always knew I was Pregnant. That was always her Q. She was angry that I was pregnant all the time. The baby I was carrying; and Jebez would be the same age for two weeks.

My sitter was the mother of two grown sons and a daughter. Another couple lived on the other side in the joining unit. They had no children, so they spoiled my little Jebez. They kept his hands full of some kind of food or fruit all the time they were home. No matter how I ask them not to do that; they never stopped until they moved.

When they moved; my sitter's daughter and husband moved in that unit. Our land lord furnished the stoves in the Units; but the oven in our unit didn't work. When I wanted to bake something, I had to go to the next street over to my sister-in-Law's whom I called; my sis, to use her oven. My husband was working at a hot factor. Sometimes I wanted to bake something. On this very hot day; I was getting very close to my delivery date. I always would get so huge with my pregnancies. I wanted to do something nice for my husband. I carried every thing over to her house I wanted to bake for our dinner. I made several trips back and forth. It was a scrumptious dinner. I thought I had done something great. When Jahari finished his dinner; he did not say thanks for all the trouble I had gone through to prepare the meal. Instead; he started an argument; and had enough nerve to threaten to hit me with a bottle because he needed an excuse to get out. That day; I looked in his eyes and said: if you lay a hand on me today; one of us is going to hell. As angry as I was: I could not see me being heaven bound. I was out of control for a moment. He really saw me; for the first time. I was tired, hot, angry, and feeling unappreciated; and I was ready to let him have it. So he left. That was what he wanted to do anyway. That was my first out of control.

I confronted the land lord about the oven. I had asked him numerous times to fix it. I was already upset with him because he had let himself into our Unit. I had not had a chance to empty my Kid's bath water from the night before; he accused me of being negligent. I was too huge to do all the work I had to do. I had to carry all the water for washing clothes and bathing the Kids. Jahari did not do anything to help out; he thought he was Mr. Pretty boy; all he did was run the streets. I was angry enough to invite the land lord for a confrontation. I told him, I would fight him until we both look like two tired coons. He asked; "how is that? I said; shitty as hell. He dropped his head and walked away. He had an arrogant disposition, and none of the tenants liked him as a land lord. He never did anything to improve the Unit while we lived there. That was my second out of control.

The Sitter's two sons would feel sorry for me and take turns helping me carry the water evenings when they would come to visit their Mom.

The water pump was a half block away. When Jahari comes home he would start an argument because they helped me; and some times we would fight. He would accuse me of being sweet on one of them. We did admire each other; but that was as far as it went. He was a handsome young man. Jahari was still drinking. One night he came home so sick from drinking; he threw up in his hat. I guess that embarrassed him to the point he stopped drinking. The kids were getting older. They did not need to see that.

The coin Refrigerator

We purchased a refrigerator from one of the Department Stores. In order to make the monthly payments' it was designed with a coin box attached to the back of the unit. Jahari got paid every two weeks. Each payday we would purchase enough quarters, and drop them in the slots. It only operated on quarters. If we did not feed it; it would not run. The salesman would come and empty the coin box once a month until the refrigerator was paid for.

We would have a grocery bill at the neighborhood grocery store every two weeks. Some times we could not pay the full bill for that period, and then it would carry over to the next pay week. We kept a running account. Our children were big eaters. I would cook the whole box of what ever I was preparing for breakfast each morning. If it was Oat meal, grits, cream of wheat, whatever; the children had hot breakfast every morning before going to school.

The baby was born while we still lived there; another girl. Because I named her what I wanted to; Big-Sis and I almost lost friendship; because she wanted to name her, but I said no! I already had her name chosen. It was Glo She was a crying baby. She would cry every night for hours. She wanted to be held, and lots of attention. The sitter was the only person who could quiet her to sleep. I had to go to work each morning. I could not hold her all night. I was changed to afternoons. The sitter was like a mother to me. I really did love having her around to talk to and help out.

After Glo was three months old I had gone to work at an Ammunition Plant. I met a young lady who worked on the line next to me. She taught me correct grammar. I would say (chunk) instead of throw. I would (gap) instead of yarn. She said to me; "you are such a beautiful and likable person. Do you mind if I correct your grammar? I was happy someone cared enough. She taught me a lots right there on that line at work.

I got pregnant again; and I was only able to work six months before someone reported it. My plan was to work as long as I could: because we were struggling financially. We traveled to work in car pools. Each person who lived in close proximity of each other took turns driving. One week when it was my turn to drive; everybody was joking and laughing. I thought I would add something to the conversation. One lady asks me to stop the car she wanted to fight. That stopped me from trying to tease. I like telling funny jokes; but I don't tease with anybody. I was told my voice sound too authoritative.

After personnel found out I was pregnant; I was terminated, that was the Company policy. They would not hire pregnant Women. They would take a urine test upon hiring. If you were pregnant; they would not hire you. It was too dangerous to work in that type of environment if you were because of the Radiation we worked in. My supervisor knew that; but she hated to see me go. We had such good relationship. I did not know the dangers of Radiation back then. I'm sure most of us didn't. I'm sure my Supervisor didn't either. I have done a lot of reading about it; and I'm very conscious about it now.

My Supervisor lived forty miles from the job. When I left the job; she gave me a beautiful baby shower at her house. Lots of the coworkers were invited and attended. I had everything the baby needed. We stayed in touch for a long time. The Ammunition part of the plant closed and it became Apsa. The young Lady who befriended me also attended the shower and gave things for the baby. She also gave me some beautiful antique furniture; a coffee table and two end tables. We drove thirty five miles to her home to pick them up. They were beautiful pieces of antique. We kept that furniture many years.

THE SECOND AFFAIR

One night the baby sitter's daughter and husband were at the club, they got into an altercation; and he cut her. I thought he was a terrible man for doing such a thing; I was very angry with him too. When ever she would be home alone I would keep an eye out for her safety; because they were separated. We thought he might try to hurt her again. I had no idea at that time; they were fighting because she was having an affair with my husband, and he had caught them together. A year later we found a house to rent. Not an apartment; a real house. It was a few miles from where we were living. The Lady owned the house who had asked me to stop the car so we could fight; rented it to us. They also lived next door. We were great neighbors. All was well. After moving there; my baby sitter stops having anything to do with me. I kept trying to contact her; but no respond. I was so hurt; she was a mother figure in my life. I never found out why she cut our ties. I kept trying to find her. I never saw or heard from her again. I heard years later that she moved to another State and was deceased.

I had the baby in January. She was child number five. We named her Maggie. Jahari's older Louie and my Sis; helped us out lots with our children. She only had one Son; and wanted more kids. She would come over and bath Maggie, dress her and take her to her house every day. We began to let her keep her as long as she wanted to. Then she began to ask us to give her to them. That went on until she was about five. Jahari might not have stayed home to help out, but he was not about to give one of his kids away. He said; "NO"! We didn't fall out and loose friendship; they continued to help out and buy things for all the kids. We really don't know what we would have done without them. Whatever they needed for school; if we could not buy it; they would make sure the kids had what they need for school. When our first child was born my sis sent a box of hand made close to us. I had not met her or Louie. That's when I started calling her my sis.

THE ANSWER TO MY SIS'S PRAYER

My sis's young sister was living with them while she was in grade school. We all called her Lil Sister. After she grew up and graduated from high school; she got pregnant and had a baby girl. That was an answer to My Sis's prayers. That helped to wean them from asking us for our baby. They raised her until Lil Sister got married and moved cross town. We purchased a lot while we lived in the rented house. Our plan was to build a house some day. Another couple bought a lot next to ours. Our lot would be across the street from a store, and next door to the store was a house where a family would move into from the City; and their Daughter would be my baby sitter. We lived in a rented house about two years. Our neighbors a beautician and family lived across the street, Louie, and my sis use to get together with them and play cards on week-ends. I never learned to play. She worked out of her home. She taught me to be her shampoo girl. She went back to School and got her Teachers License in Cosmetology. I call her the Teacher. Doing the summer my niece or my cousin would visit. This cousin was auntie's daughter. The niece was my sister's daughter. They would keep the kids while I help out in her Shop.

THE POLIO SCARE

Little Jebez was one of my bed wetter. He was not school age yet. Every morning he would call out to me asking if he may get up. Sometimes I would not be ready for him to get up. I would need them to sleep while I get my house work done: because I was an early riser. Finally I said yes. He kept asking; I kept saying yes. After about the firth time; I went in to see why he never got up. I stood him on his feet, but he could not stand on his legs. I panicked; we only had one car, and Jahari was at work. I called Big Sister and we rushed him to the ER. Our Doctor met us there and diagnosed him with polio. We were devastated. Further testing by him found that not to be the case. We never found out what happen to his legs. Thank God it wasn't Polio. He never had any more problems with his legs.

17.
Mother Returns

MOTHER WAS READY TO come back to live with us. Jahari went south to get her. He and my mother got along fine. Jahari was really great to her.

She was still having some type of Spells. It would take five people to hold her down when the attacks occurred. We would call the neighbors to assist us. The spells continued for months. Jahari decided it was time to start building the house on our property we had purchased. His two brothers and the guys he worked with helped build the house. After we moved into our house; it really was not large enough, but it was a start. We had no closets or storage space. We eventually added a couple rooms but no closets. We still had to carry water for everything; and still had out door toilets. I had my last two babies while we lived there. They were born at the same Hospital as Jebez.

I always had a full week. My work was never done. Mondays were laundry day. We were blessed to purchase a used washing machine. I was trying to breast feed Rae and feed clothes through the washing machine ringer at the same time. The baby's blanket got caught in the ringer and rolled her into the machine. The dasher was washing the clothes. I snatched Rae from that washer so fast; her blanket never got wet. I never tried that again.

Tuesdays and Wednesdays I ironed. It would take two days to iron an average of thirty five dresses, not counting the men's shirts and pants. I even starched and ironed their play clothes. Thursday was general house cleaning day, and Friday was grocery shopping. I was ironing one day; my mom started in on me about being pregnant again. She snatched the dress I was ironing off the ironing board, threw it on the floor and did the roach dance on it. We did not have carpet on the floor, so that garment had to be laundered again. I felt like committing suicide. I was silly enough to think that would ease my pain. I thought about the many ways I could do it. I felt as though that was my only way out. I thought about getting the ladder and putting it against the house; and go up on top of the house and jump off. She was always on my case about something. I was frustrated about my life. I was always pregnant and never had any recreations. I only saw my husband when it was time to eat, go to bed, fix his lunch, and leaving for work.

Mother traveled back and forth from Mississippi to Illinois. When she would get angry with her relatives down south; she would call for Jahari to come get her. She would stay with us a while; and when she gets angry with me; he had to take her back. That went on for four years. She finally had a nervous break down.

Our Doctor had to admit her to a mental hospital. She was there for about eighteen months. We never missed a visit. The staff would tell us that was the key to her recovery. When family show interest, to anyone who is incarcerated, that causes the staff to take better care of them because it shows some one cares about them. They complemented us for being so faithful and caring.

Soon as she was able to go out on the grounds, we would take lunches and have a picnic with her. She loved her grand children after they got here and began to grow up. She just didn't think I should have had so many. After they grew older; she and her grand's were inseparable. After my mother was home a while; it started all over again her wanting to go back and forth. She had two sisters; and one brother still living down south.

Jahari didn't mind the trips back and forth. I found out that he had a Mistress down there. While we were married; he fathered two other daughters. They were the same ages as our last two daughters. One daughter's mother was my baby sitter's daughter. The other another daughter lived in Mississippi. I was told by Jahari's sister that we were separated at the time the one in Mississippi was born. Never the less we were still married.

THE ACCIDENT

On a Sunday afternoon we were all in the car going to the park I was about seven months pregnant with Ann. She was my eight pregnancy and the last. We were hit head on by an on coming car. One car was turning; and had stopped; with signal light blinking. The car behind him was going too fast to stop; so he went around him and hit us. The Ambulance was called for me. They were told I was pregnant. They insisted that I go for observation. I was uncomfortable because I had not ever been close to an Ambulance. When the nurse put me on the examining table; my bra was so raggedy; I had it tied up on me. The nurse asks; "What have we here? I was so embarrassed; I did not answer. I would always say; one day I will buy some clothes for me when the kids grow up. I was ok and was released to go home. We all were so blessed that day. My mother was not with us; she was back in Ms.

One other time we had gone to the City to visit Jahari's cousin. The kids were fighting in the back seat. He reached back to spank one of them and ran into the back of a car. No one was hurt. We use to drive to Chicago every blue moon to get white castles. They only cost eight cents then. Those two accidents caused Maggie to fear riding in an automobile for quite a while. She said; "she would never drive" but that changed; when she got older and went off to collage.

MY DOCTORS WARNING

My Doctor began to warn us that I needed to stop having babies. My blood was beginning to get out of control. He said it could be very dangerous, because with the last two pregnancies; my blood pressure was too high, and we could not get it under control. He also said, "Toxemia could set in at delivery". He would send me to bed; but I could not rest in bed with five or six children. He advised that I needed to have my tubes tied. My husband did not want me to do that. My intention was to have it done before the last pregnancy, but the rule at the hospital was you had to wait sis weeks. When my six weeks was up I was pregnant again. After that baby, the law had changed. I could have it done before being released. In order to have my tubs tied; I needed Jahari to sign the papers. I had to threaten him that I would yell to the top of my voice right in that hospital if he did not sign. He did sign the papers, and I had the surgery. He knew I would carry out my threat. I had been pregnant eight times by the time I was twenty two. One was a miscarriage. I think it a miscarriage; one of my brother-in-law's had gotten some pills for me at my request; and I took them, weeks latter it happened. All the other seven were healthy and happy babies. I was happy to know I would not be pregnant again. I thought Jahari would be home with us more, but I was wrong. His lie was; he stayed gone because I was pregnant all the time. What was the excuse then; I was not pregnant any more. He talked like I was getting pregnant by myself.

Two of the fellow's who helped Jahari build the house had wives who were very flirtatious. They were two sister-in-laws. Jahari and his two brothers were always at their house. We would sometimes visit them with our husbands. Ammie was light complexion; she was bolder than her sister-in-law Ella. She was darker complexion. Ammie had a habit; sitting with her legs open in front of our husbands. We wives never found out if they had an affair with all three brothers; but Jahari had an affair with Ammie. The community had a dance to raise money to try to get sewer in our neighborhood I was so happy to get a chance to go. After a while, I missed my husband from the crowd. I began to look every where for him. He was not there. Amy's husband sister told me Jahari had eased out from the dance and had gone to Amy's house. Amy's husband was at the dance with us. I began to drink all the whisky I could get. I was so hurt. I wanted to get drunk. I seceded. When Jahari returned, the dance was ending. He had to help me to the car. I cried so hard and told him what he had done. He never said a word. I wanted him to deny it.

We all began to visit each other pretty regular. Ella was very hilarious; she would keep us laughing. She was a great seamstress. She could make anything. Ella's husband name was Ed. He told me that Jahari was also having an affair with his wife too. I never said anything to either one of them about what I suspected. Ella's husband started asking me if he and I could have an affair. He was not appealing to me at all. He was short fat and ball. But I still did not have any clothes. I had seen a gold corduroy suit in a catalog. I wanted that suit so much. I would gaze at it and imagine me in it, but I had no way of purchasing it. I guess he wanted revenge. . I told him if he would buy it for me I would go out with him. He said he would. I ordered the suit and he paid for it. I kept my promise. He continued to pursue me, but he just wasn't my cup of tea. I had not ever cheated on Jahari. I always had some legit excuses, not to be with Ed again. I could be a convincing liar when it came to making excuses to men. I guess I was looking for revenge too. I did not have any money to buy anything I needed or wanted

My sis and I got a job at a department store down town where they made coats. Big sis and I had gone to School and taken some sewing classes. The Employers could purchase material from the store at a discount. I purchased two pieces and made myself two skirts. I purchased two turtle neck tea shirt. I wore them every where I went unless I borrowed something from my sis. I was raised not to borrow anything;. The store closed so we were out of work.

I always liked sleeping late. So when the kids went to school, most times I would go back to bed. Amy would call me every morning; waking me up; acting like she was my friend and wanting to talk. I think she just wanted to see if I knew anything about her and Jahari. One morning she called and woke me up from my sleep. She caught me on my bad side that morning. I let her have it. I told her; I know you are going with my husband and don't call here again waking me up! She did not know what to say: she just hung up the phone. She never called again. I saw her years later; and she looked like a witch.

18.

My Brother Going to Prison

I FOUND OUT THAT my brother had moved to City. I had a phone call that he was in jail for a robbery he had committed. I was concern about him; but I was afraid to drive in the City. My husband asked our neighbor the Teacher's husband to take me up to my brother's hearing. He did not want to take off work to take me. Our neighbor was off on sick leave. We left early that morning; we arrived at the court house by the time it opened. They did not bring my brother before the Judge until late that evening. We had sat there all day. When the guards finally brought him in; the Public Defender asks for a continuance until the next day. I could not go back the next day. Our neighbor told Jahari that his wife said we were not at the court house all that time. She accused us of being some place else. I could not believe that; because Jahari would get calls all times of the night or day when he was on sick leave with a back injury. He would rush her to the Veteran Hospital. Her husband was in and out the hospital regular. Some times he would already be in the hospital and his wife would get a call to come quick at midnight. Jahari would get out of bed and take her there. There were times we thought we were going to loose him. The hospital was at least thirty five miles or more from where we lived.

When the trial ended; brother was sentenced to five years in Statesville. I went to visit him every visiting day. I loved my brother. The prison was close to where I lived. When he had been there about four years; he was assigned to work release. I could visit him outside;

and have a picnic type visit. I enjoyed visiting him. That is where I got to know him. He was very intelligent. I would enjoy hearing him explain every verse of the Lord's Prayer. I had never heard it explained that way; and I have not ever heard any one do it since. When he was released he went back to the City and later got married. I lost contact with him again. He was a rolling stone. Wherever he lay his hat was his home.

THE DREAM

Jahari had been off work about nine months with his back problem. After returning back to the work; he decided to quit working at the Factory and started to work at a Gas and Service station. I was working at a Restaurant. The owner of the Restaurant and his wife also worked along with Ms. Mary and me. Ms. Mary was an eldely lady; old enough to be retired. The Boss was always feeling on my rear. Ms Mary and I were so afraid that his wife was going to see him doing that. When the shift end each evening; he would take us home and make me be the last to take home. Some time he and I would have to wait for the boat to go through the canal. We talked while we waited. That bridge was a swing bridge that was level with the Street. All the other bridges would open up from the top. He seemed to like that street, because it was not traveled much. That time of the evening, most likely; we would be the only ones waiting. While we were waiting one evening; fear came over me. I thought: this man could throw me into this river and no one would know what happened to me. I was thinking about quitting the job because of his behavior.

Ms. Mary came in to work one morning with her hand all bandaged up. I asked her what happen. She said; "she dream that the boss's wife was after me with a knife; and she was trying to protect me from her; and hit her hand on the trunk beside her bed and cut it". That dream was too real. I knew it was time for me to quit that job; and I did. Then I went to work doing house cleaning. The lady I was working for; husband was a great Surgeon. He saved a baby's life by during surgery to correct its intestines. The baby was born with its stomach up side down. They adopted the baby. Some times I would be holding the baby and his excuse to feel on me was to pretend he was playing with the baby. I had worked for them about two years before they adopted the baby. They had two other beautiful children in elementary school. I really liked working for her; because she was simple. She did not have all that extravagant stuff for me to dust and clean. She said; "what her neighbors had did not bother her. She just liked comfort".

Loosing Our Heater

We had purchased a large coal heater from one of the department stores. It kept the house warm all night. All we had to do was get up once during the night to put more coal in. Three of the kids were bed wetter's. We needed heat all night and into the mornings when the kids get up to wash up for school, even though they had their baths the night before. We had had the heater about two years. Jahari had stop making payments on it. The store was threatening to repossess it. I didn't know what we were going to do. I was not making enough money doing day work to catch up the payments. When I got to work Doc's wife had gone to the beauty shop. He and I were in the kitchen. He was having coffee and I was cleaning up the dishes. He asks me if I was ok. I guess my problems were showing on my face. They always do. I try to hide them, but they show though. I told him about the heater and that the company was threatening to repossess it; and that I had a house full of children. He asks; "How much is owed" I told him; and he offered the money to pay for it. I accepted; and paid him back the way he- wanted his pay. I paid for the heater and I soon quit working there too.

Jahari Still Chasing

Jahari was still chasing women; and now one of his woman's husband started trying to hit on me. He thought if he told me about another woman Jahari was seeing; that would give him a chance with me. He had tried every other way; His wife was the one who would call and wake me every morning. He told me where the woman lived and how I could catch them together. He told me when Jahari leaves the house; all I had to do was follow him over on the next street. He wanted to pay him back for going with his wife. Every one seemingly wanted revenge. I pretended I was not listening to what he was saying; but I was all ears. I thought: the nerve of them; right under my nose. That same night; Jahari said; "he was going to gas up the car so we could go see my mother". She was back in the mental hospital. The two boys ask if they may go with him. He said; "you don't need to go". Those were his favorite words. I asked why they can't go. You always tell them they don't need to go. He replied; "they just don't need to go" I knew something was up. I thought about what the man had told me.

My Aunt's oldest daughter was visiting us for the summer. She would come some summers to stay with the children while I work. It was a little cool that evening, she had a sweater wrap around her shoulders. When Jahari left; I grab the sweater off her shoulder and ran through the alley to the next street. That is where the man had told me the woman lived. There they were. (Right under my nose) He was picking the woman up at her house on the corner. She came to the car; said something to Jahari, and ran inside to got a sweater, ran back out, got in the car and slid right under him where I usually sit when I was in the car with him. He had a 1957 Chrysler, yellow and black, with duel pipes. You could hear those pipes at a distance. He kept it clean and shining. They pass right by me. I was standing in a drive-way that had just been poured with fresh rocks. I was so hurt: I was frozen; I could not move nor throw a rock. I stood and watched as they hesitated; as if they were deciding where they were going to go. As they drove out of sight; I went back home. I said nothing to my cousin. I had said that I was not going to say a word when he returned. But he seems as if he was so- happy. I could not hold my piece; I confronted him.

He lied; I told him that I had seen him. He took me into the bed room, so the kids would not hear, and we lay across the bed. He kept lying; he said; "he was picking her up for a friend". I knew he was lying; he did not associate with friends. I told him; what ever anybody tells you they saw me doing; it will be true. That I was no longer going to sit by while he is out chasing women. I said if it was that much fun; I needed some fun in my life. "He asks me not to do that; but he still would not confess the truth about what I had just seen. I can forgive anything if you tell me the truth. I hate lying with a passion.

When someone lies about a situation, you know they have no intention of repentance. There are three spirits that travel together; they are: lying, stealing and murder. They follow very close together and they are very dangerous spirits.

JAHARI SETS ME UP

My oldest Daughter Louise was mature enough to be with the kids for a few hours; and my cousin was still visiting with us. When Jahari would leave home, I would leave home too. When he comes home; I would not be there on purpose. I was trying to show him what it felt like when he is out late at night. He began to get jealous. He thought I was out with some one. Some one had told him that I was seeing a person who was a member of our church. They told him his name; and Jahari called the man's wife, and told her that I was out with her husband right now; as they speak. She said; "I know she is not out with him right now; my husband is at home getting ready for work because he works midnights". I was at our neighbor's house drilling her for her Cosmetology Teacher's exam that she would be taking in a few weeks. I was there until two o'clock in the A: M. She only lived on the next street behind our house. I did not want him to know where I was. I was trying to show him how it feels when your spouse is out, and you don't have a clue where they are.

That next day the lady had her husband take her by the Service Station where Jahari worked to confront him about the call. I don't know what they talked about but when they left him; they came to our house to confront me. They pulled into our drive-way and blew the horn. I went out to their car. She told what had transpired; I was shocked. We talked; and they left. My husband could have gotten me killed. The church where we all went was small, and would be packed every Sunday. Everybody would gather at the door trying to get out at the same time. She could have easily stabbed me there in the door way, and no one would have seen who did it. I lost lots of respect for Jahari after that. I never called anybody on him, nor wanted to hurt him. I just wanted him to stop chasing. There is a scripture that say; "you will reap what you sow; whether it's good or bad".

19.

I Began To Cheat

I KNEW MOST OF the women Jahari went out with. I never threatened any of them. There was a guy who kept telling My sis and big-sis that he wanted to talk to me. I said no for a long time. I finally let them talk me into just going to hear what he wanted to talk about. I was not dumb; I knew what he wanted. After they kept on saying talking can't hurt; I finally did go and have the talk. It ended up the way I knew it would. We saw each other for a while. I got so bold; I would walk right up the street and get into his car. I really did not care if Jahari found out. I thought that would make him stop chasing women. I became infatuated with the guy. I began to think I was madly in love with the man. I soon came to my senses. I really did love my husband. That infatuation soon vanished; but he would call me some times just to say hello.

One day Jahari was cutting the grass, and I was on the phone talking to him. He threw that lawn mower down; ran into the house and tried to make me tell him who I was talking to. I hung up the phone and the fight begun. Jahari beat me up so bad that day; I almost lost my eye. The kids were screaming and crying. A few weeks went by the eye was not getting any better; his brother told him; "he'd better take me to the doctor to see about it; that I could loose it". But he would not take me. It still was not getting any better; I called the guy; and asked him to pick something up for my eye from the pharmacy, and throw it over the fence. He did; I got it and used it. It helped, and my eye soon got ok. I had to teach Louise to help with the cooking until I got better.

That beating only made me want to pay him back for what he had done to me. When Jahari would leave the house I would be sitting by the heater on a stool. When he leaves I would leave. When he return I would be sitting on that same stool. He would ask; "you still sitting on that stool? I would say yep; I am still sitting here; I would have gone; and done my thing, and back home. My conscious started to get the best of me; I decided that was wrong. Two wrongs don't ever make a right. I knew Jesus was not pleased with that. I repented and got back in church and made my piece with God. I made sure that the children were in Sunday school every Sunday. Ms. May was over the youth. She always kept them busy; working in the church. Every holiday there were some types of program for the children. Easter was her greatest affair. The older kids sang in the youth choir, and the little ones had their own little choir. One Sunday of each month her little babies would all sing together. Ages from five down to if they could walk and talk. She was in love with all the children. She didn't care how young they were; she would find something for them to do.

Jahari sang in a quartet group he really could sing and play the Guitar. That's where he met most of his women. I loved to hear him sang. I was singing in the senior choir. Jebez learned to play Guitar as an inheritance from his dad. Also the two baby girls, and the elder son. They inherited their singing from Jahari. I quit singing and lost my voice because of sinus problems.

THE BIG PROMISE

The couple next door; Jahari and I went out to a club one Saturday night to have a few drinks and dance. I loved dancing. We never had gone out dancing or any type of recreations after we got married. We had been married ten years. This was our first time of going out together except to church. I thought that was a start toward us working on our marriage. While we were there, it was announced that M W was going to be at the Coliseums in the following month. Our husbands promised to take us. I was so excited; I rushed that month in. That was something I was looking forward to. I was so excited that my husband was starting to take me places. He was so much fun to be with. He really was a comedian. Two of his children took after him. Glo and Jebez look just like him and keep you laughing like him.

When that weekend finally arrived; I was set and ready to go. When Jahari came in from work around 2:15 a.m.; I told him how excited I was about our night out. He said we are not going to the Coliseum tonight; because I have to work tomorrow. I was so disappointed. I said to him; Big-Sis is going, I can go with her. I also reminded him; whenever he went out it didn't matter whether he had to work the next day; why does it matter now? If you are not going; why can't I go with her? He said; **<u>"YOU AINT GOING NO WHERE".</u>** He left to go to the store to get something for lunch. When he left; I called Big Sis and told her to pick me up over at Jahari's brother's house. His brother never said a word. He was a Pastor, but he knew I stayed home too much and needed a break from the kids.

I borrowed clothes from his wife, My Sis got dressed and big sis picked me up and we went to the Coliseum. I was so popular that night; all the guys wanted to know; who is the new girl on the block. I really had a good time. I met a lot of people. I felt like I wanted to be single. I had never been told that I was pretty. I stayed pregnant every year. Who is pretty pregnant? But I tried to look my best. I purchased myself three maternity outfits. I kept my hair beautiful. I wore my make-up every day; I had a head full of my own hair, I wore my high heel shoes every day. My kids were immaculate, their hair was neat, my house was clean, Jahari's dinner was ready every day at two fifteen, and the sex was regular. I watched the soaps every day. The actors wore heels and looked beautiful. I was silly enough to think that was the real world; so I copied after them and it worked. By the time I realized that was just a sitcom; I was already in the habit. I kept it up. I think it was a positive habit. I never did let it go; and it became natural for me. Jahari would ask me; "where you have been? He finally got use to it.

I was twenty seven before I knew what an orgasm was. My friends laughed at me when the conversation came up between us ladies one day. They were going on about what it felt like. After listening a while; I ask; what are you guys talking about. They teased me because I had seven children; and did not know what they were talking about. They said to me; you really don't know what we are talking about do you? I really didn't know. They could not explain it to me: because I found out it is un-explainable. That was something I would have to experience for myself.

When big sis dropped me off at home; it was around two o'clock a.m. I eased into the house; and took My-Sis's clothes off at the door, because I thought we would have another fight; but everyone was sleeping. I took the hammer and got in bed with one of the kids. I had made up my mind that I was not taking any more butt whippings. When Jahari got up for work that morning; he came into the room; and said; "didn't I tell you not to go any where last night". I said; yes you did; but I did nothing wrong. I get tired of being home all the time' just the children and me. You don't ever take me any place. I had a nice time; although I thought Jahari might step through the door anytime to hall me out that door.

THE BRAKE UP

Jahari said to me: I'm going to fix it so you can go and come when you get ready. I was so- happy! I was still doing day work. On that Friday he picked me up from work; and said to me. "I am picking up my check today; and it will be up to you whether I give my resignation". I ask; what do you mean? "He said unless you can do better; I am leaving". I said if you think staying at home all the time; while you're always in the streets; and not ever taking me any place; **NO!** I can't do any better. He said ok; and he resigned from his job that Friday. He packed his clothes and left. As he drove away Jebez ran behind the car hollering and crying and begging his daddy not to leave him. He never stopped the car to try to explain anything to him. Jebez was going to be nine years old in two months. A few hours later Jahari called back long distance and asks that same Question; and I gave the same answer. I was happy that he was gone. I was getting ready to enjoy a new life

A few weeks later he came back to town and convinced me to go with him to counseling with our pastor. We went to counsel. If the Pastor had told me what God said about divorce; I probably would have considered staying and being miserable with him. But the Pastor skipped that part; so I had no need to reconcile and continue living that way. I found out later that God said I could get a divorce for the cause of fornication. I was ok anyway. Then I found out that fornication and adultery are two different things. So I was kind of straddling the fence about the divorce, until I read that He said; I can be forgiven for everything; except blaspheme against the Holy Ghost. I realized Jahari would not have changed. I saw his life style as the years passed. Jahari and I eventually lived in the same City. There was no change. Those brothers had (what I call the can't help its.) Women were their down fall. God said; there is forgiveness for <u>everything</u>; except <u>not accepting Jesus in my heart</u>; and He was already there.

Jahari really called himself teaching me a lesson; but it back-fired on him. He sent every one who was willing to talk to me; to see if I would change my mind and get back together with him. People were really shocked to hear that we were broke up. We were married twelve years. I was twenty six years old when we separated, he was thirty one. That was such a petty thing to break up over. I have never regretted that we went our separate ways; because I would not have been able to live under those circumstances and be a whole person.

When Jahari and I; would go to the grocery store; and to church, or even when taking me to work. I would ride right under him. Cars didn't have bucket seats then. You could sit right under your man. On Sundays he would take us to the flowing well; and there was always a Concession Stand there. They sold peanuts, candy, and hot dogs. That is the only place he would take us. Every Sunday afternoon; he took us there. When ever he and I were in the car together; People would say it looked as if only one person was there. I would be in the middle, and one of the older kids would sit near the door. Of course the doors were always locked to protect the kids. After Jahari and I did not reconcile through Counseling; he moved in with a very attractive young lady over on the next street behind our house. She and I would run into each other at the clubs periodically. She would not speak to me, but I was always friendly to her; she showed me respect, and I respected her. I knew her family. She was just a kid.

JAHARI GOT ILL

Jahari's Family and I remained connected. They are really the only family I have. We grew up in the same house together; I was just a kid when Jahari and I moved in with his family. His baby Sister and I really became very close. She lived with us a while after we moved into our house. They informed me that Jahari was in the hospital and that the doctor could not find out what was wrong. His eyes were red; they thought it was Yellow-Jaundice. They transferred him to a City hospital.

I went with his family to see him. I was concerned about him. To my surprise he told me some years later; my coming to visit him made it worse: because it was our break-up he was grieving over; and that he had cried so much; that's why his eyes were red. All he needed to do; was tell me he loved me. I never heard that word come from him; and tell me he was going to try to change his way of thinking about control. Pride would not let him do that. All I wanted was to be a family; and do some things together just him and me; not just having babies.

A man has it wrong. They think the only submission is on the woman's part. That is not true. The word says; likewise you younger people submit yourselves to your elders, <u>yes all of you</u> be submissive to one another, and be clothed with humility. 1st pet 5:5. He is talking to all of the children of God. It takes communication to do that. I am not trying to say that I did not play a part in our braking up. We were very young when we got married. We had no one to guide or teach us anything about love and relationship. His dad knew nothing about love and relationships. He raised hell every day about something. My dad was always raising hell too. Some men think women are their property instead of companion. Stubbornness comes out of pride. We think our way is best, or at least we want others to think that, so we refuse to give in. Stubbornness is being unyielding, refusing to move, and refusing to change. It is hardened resistance to others or to God himself. Not only that, stubbiness usually keeps us from doing what is best for us, and in the end we hurt ourselves. I was stubborn too. If we don't know the purpose of a thing; we have a tendency to abuse it.

JAHARI LEFT THE STATE

After Jahari pulled himself together; he left the State again. He went back to His home town. I received no support from him for the children. We had to turn to the State for help. I would ask my case workers if there was any way that the state could send me to Beauty School. They would all tell me no; they had no such plan. So I was a stay home Mom. No matter what the case worker said; or how they tried to push me out to work away from my babies; I was determined to stay close to them. When she ask have you been job looking. I would say; <u>no</u>! I will not leave my kids. They were still small. I am all they have. Three of the kids were bed wetters. I was a bed wetter as a child; and I understood what that was like. I was patient with them. The children had to carry water for everything. We manage to keep every thing clean and smelling fresh. Everybody had chores, that way it wasn't too hard to keep everything in place. When God give us children; it is our responsibility to be with them and to raise them the way they should go from us. We can't raise them by being away from them eight hours day. Out of the seven children; nobody ever had to come back home. No babies out of wedlock from the girls. My boys needed that moral male figure. Some boys do well without it. My boys didn't. They brought me much heart ache.

I'm writing this book to tell some one; no matter how tough the going gets; with your hand in God's hand you can make it. He never said that if you belong to Him you would not have afflictions. He said we would have many; <u>BUT;</u> He would deliver us from <u>ALL</u> of them. You don't have to <u>LOOK LIKE</u> what you been through.

The neighbor next door spreaded vicious lies about me because; I put him in his place. I told him; in the first place, we are neighbors, second place, your wife is my friend, and I do not go with my friend's man. He got so angry he went to his job and told people that I stay out all night from my kids; and that you could not get into my house because of the filth. He said my house was so nasty you would not want to come there.

My brother-in-law who was a Pastor worked at the same plant. He defended me. He said; "I don't know about her staying out all night; but she is an immaculate house keeper. He said; "her kids wet the bed every night, but I have never smelled any urine odors in her house". He said; "my wife and I have wondered how she does it with no running water". That lie was silenced. No tongue could rise against me. My oldest daughter was such great help to me. We worked as a team. She would help me bath the kids. I began to realize that when I talk to her about different things; she under-stood. I started early telling them about the birds and bees. I explain to them; their body only belongs to their husbands and wives. I talk to my boys too. I did not let them be dumb as I was; growing up. The boys did not listen. But now they wish they had. I told the girls, don't always be available at the parties. No matter how much you would like to be there; allow the guys to miss you. I taught them when a young man come to pick them up; don't allow him to blow for you. He must come to the door, speak to me and walk you to the car. The same when he comes to bring you home. Walk you to the door. No man wants to see his girl always at the place every time the doors open. They grew up to be one man woman. They just choose the wrong men. They all married men who love to fight; except Louse. He did not fight her; but he did not realize what a jewel he had until it was too late. That curse just seemed to follow down the generations, if you don't break it. What I'm saying is break that curse of allowing abuse to hang on to you. That's what I saw growing up; that's what they saw; and we didn't know how to break it.

We heated our bath water, and took baths in a tin tub every day. The girl's bath in the same water first. They would dump their water and heat more water; then the boys would bathe. Jebez's teachers became very concern about his voice. She got in touch with the Catholic administration where a Sister got involved with the therapy. She was so concern about his voice. We started therapy for him which went on a few years. Jebez was nine years old when the therapy began. Big Sis made sure we never missed an appointment. I did not have a car, but she did. We went back and forth to the City to the children's hospital until he was thirteen. Finally the Doctors all agreed that Jebez had nasals growing on his vocal cords and that they would operate at age fifteen. When He reached fifteen they said it was psychological and that he could be experiencing something concerning his Dad. It could have been something I took; trying to abort him. His voice never changed. True confession is good for the soul. We do stupid things in this life. But God is a forgiving God when we repent to him and others.

20.
Getting Back Together

I WAS TWO WEEKS away from my first check; with public Assistant; when Jahari came back to town. He talked me into getting back together with him. I reported to the Public Aid that he had come back home; so that stopped them from processing the application. I had met a John-Doe who had been helping us out with money for heat and food. I did not have a shed to lock my heating Coal in; people would steal it. I could call him; and he would bring money so I could order more Coal for us. Then Jon-doe decided to give me an allowance every week. I asked Jahari to give me a chance to tell him what was happening in private; before he comes home that evening, Jahari promised he would wait until about nine o'clock before coming. John-Doe had become more than just a friend. I wanted the chance to break it off gentle. I wasn't in love; I just wanted to be able to explain in private; that I was not just using him; because I don't know what we would have done without him. It was no need for Jahari to know who he was. He had not contributed anything to help us since he left. I did a little hair for my friends and that help put food on the table. But for the most part the allowance that John-doe gave helped carried the load. I would work at a few restaurants; but they did not pay enough to hire a sitter.

I had a couple of baby sitters. One of them was a tall stocky lady. She was very sweet, but she had a problem with her hygiene. The kids would tell me how bad she smelled. Where ever she would sit on the couch; would smell so bad I had to let her go. I found another sweet little lady; she met all my needs, but my elder son kept her busy. One day he went up in the loft to tear the girl's dolls up. He and Jebez were always tearing up their dolls. This day he fell down and tore the whole sheet of sheet rock down on top of him. That scared her so much: When I got home; she begged me not to whip him. I had to try to work to feed my kids when the opportunity presented itself. The pay was so small by the time I pay the sitter, it was gone. That is why I encourage kids to get an education. I realized that was not worth me leaving my kids for.

Six weeks was a long time to be cold and hungry with seven kids and John-doe saw to it that we were warm and had food. Jahari did not give me that chance to speak to my friend alone. He was already there when John-doe; called at seven o'clock. I could not be candid with my explanation to him. I guess I was acting a little dry toward Jahari. So he said if that guy means that much to you; I will leave. It wasn't that he meant that much to me. It was just that Jahari did not respect my wishes. When something is bothering me I can't hide it. He did not give our getting back together a chance. So he packed and left again. I had to go back to the Public Assistance and re-apply for help. Only two weeks had passed, we only had to wait four weeks to get it re-started. John-Doe gambled across the street every week end. It was no problem to see him and let him know that I needed his help again. He came back to my aide.

My mother was back with us. John-Doe had rented a house over on the next street. He set it up as a night club. He hired me as his bartender just on week ends. I worked mid-nights. I only sold drinks up stairs and he did whatever they did down stairs. I would not see him until closing, when he would come up stairs to pay me. He hired a one man band. He could play three instruments at one time. Pretty soon he started asking me for a date. I could not see myself dating him. He didn't care how he dressed. He was clean; but dressed country. I found out later you don't judge a book by its cover.

Somebody called John-Doe's wife; and told her that I was running the club; and that I was having an affair with her husband. The wife called me; told me what she had heard. She said; "that this person described me to a tee". They told her how I wore my hair, and everything that they could remember about me. She said; "I would know you when I see you". I told her all I did was wait on the customers, and go home when the club closes. I ask her if she worked. She said; "no" I said whoever told you that could be jealous of you because you are a lady of leisure. She said; "maybe" I think I assured her that I was not having an affair with her husband. I quit the job and stop communication with him. That scared me that some one had given her so much detailed information about me.

I was in the Legion one night; and she put her hand in my hair and spoke to me; and said; "I told you I would know you when I see you". She was coming off as being friendly. That really scared me. I did not stay there very long. I left and went to another club. She was a very attractive tall heavy set Lady. During that time I wore my hair cut very short in back, and pushed high in top. Not a strand out of place. People would describe me as, the lady with the pretty hair. If some one was trying to describe me to someone else; that is how I was made known to that person. I thought that was cool until that incident.

When I was a child I prayed for long hair. My mother would shampoo it and let it dry and then comb it. I would scream and be all down under her legs. When I was nine I started taking care of my own hair and burned it out. We would get this book in the mail that sold everything for black people. They even sold hair extensions. She would order hair oils from them. When I became of age; I ordered a piece of hair and secured it on my head. I always knew how to style hair. Nobody ever knew it was not mine. Not even Jahari. Doing my pregnancies my hear grew nice and long. By then short hair was in. Jahari did not want me to cut it, so I would have the teacher clip a little at a time. Because I was her shampoo girl I did not have to pay. One day I got bold, and went to the barber shop and really got it cut. I did not know Jahari liked it until we separated. He told other people he liked it; not me.

When his dad got ill and was in a coma; I went to Mississippi to see him, and to be of support to Jahari. He had said to some people who were at the hospital with their family, that his wife was coming down, and she has a sharp hair cut. They told me what he said about my hair; and said; "he didn't lie; your hair is pretty". A couple years later; a relative came to visit us; she wore wigs. I went to the City with her. We went into a beauty salon to see if they could style her wig that same day. While we waited; I tried on some wigs and got hooked. I have worn them ever sense. Being a Beautician, They were easier to maintain. I liked how I could wear most colors, length, and style. My customers would say we never know what you are going to look like when we come into the shop. They loved it. They enjoyed my different looks. So did I.

I Started To Party

I ask God's permission to watch over me, and please let me go out and just dance. I had never done anything; that young people do. It's not that I think He gave me permission; I think it was my honesty, and He knows our heart already. I knew that I would be separated from Him while I was sinning; because sin is a stench in His nostrils. I would prey every day asking God; please don't let me stay out there too long. I didn't want to be lost. I just liked dancing. He really doesn't mind us dancing as long as we change partners.

When I got saved at the age of twelve; I saw so much hypocrisy, that I was confused, and I was determined that I would not be a hypocrite. People were acting as if God did not see what they were doing. Then they would say; "God understand". So I asked permission. God watched over me. No weapon formed against me prospered. They tried; but the Angels really did watch over me. Of course other sins followed the dancing. Sin is not going to be isolated. Don't ever think you can do a little sin and control all of it. The old saying is; if you let him ride, then he will want to drive. He will if you don't watch out. I became very permissive. Some things I did because I needed to; some I didn't want to; and some I didn't know how to say no.

I went into a grocery store to shop one afternoon. I never had shopped there before. It was out of my area. A tall dark man approached me and asks if he may call me. I ask; are you married. He said no. I gave him my number. Big sis and I would investigate every man we met. We became like private eyes. We had so much fun. She and I act like kids. If we met a guy one day; by the next day we knew everything about him. So we found out he was not married, but did have a girl friend. Big Sis and I enjoyed life. Her kids and my kids were like sisters and brothers. They call me Ant Mag. All the kids did.

The guy calls a few times and we talk on the phone. He invited me down to his apartment one week-end. He said; he and the girl friend were broke up. After that visit; we started seeing each other. Some body tells the girl friend, and she starts calling my house. At first I was nice; but I was working mid-nights; and the calls kept coming. I tried to tell her I was trying to sleep. But she kept calling. I got rude. I said a few terrible words to her that I will probably have to reap some day; and left the phone off the hook. I went to his place one Friday night. We were in the bedroom talking; and we herd someone pecking on the window by the bed. Big Sis had let me use her car; but I had parked the car over on the next street. He thought if he ignores her pecking she would leave. He did not own a car' but she knew he was home. She beat and called him names for a while; then pretended to have left. I got dressed; and was opening the door to go out; she rushed in as I open the door. She took off after me. I ran so fast; I thought the wind was carrying me. I use to out run all the boys when I was a kid. I still had it.

Seeing she could not catch me; as he tried to look out to see if I was ok. She double back in on him and cut him. I read about it the next day in the papers. Both were much older than I was. I guess that is what upset her so much. I did not see him any more. But later in years the lady took a liking to me. She worked in the Legion where we all hung out. I did not trust her to serve me drinks. Her sister and I became club members of a Social club

The Sweet-Heart of our club was a male name Mr. Turner. We gave many dances for Charity. I stayed in the club a few years. Some of the club members were my customers.

Two of my girl friends and I would go to the Legion on week ends. That's where I met the Love of my dreams. I started calling him Mr. Dream. He would come by the house when ever he could find a ride. He still lived at home with his parents, and didn't have a job or a car. He was a mama's boy. He was three years younger than I. I was paranoid; because back then people talked when the female was older than the male. Especially if he was spoil and didn't work. For a while; he was the kind of guy I had dreamed about. He taught me how to do the latest dances. A dance called the Madison was very popular at that time. Every body was doing it. He would take me to the dance classes at the Legion. All the ladies like dancing with him. He was very popular; and could glide over the floor like a rubber ball. I finally had met some-one who like taking me out with him. He liked showing me off. I was so happy, and hungry for attention. I had not ever had that kind of attention. I really liked being with him. He was very smart, and fun to be with. It wasn't that he couldn't get a job; he was just a spoiled brat at home with mom and dad. I did not want his family to know he was seeing me; a lady with seven kids- They were up scale people; and I was afraid to meet them. Mother left and went back south because she didn't like Mr. Dream for me. Really no one did. I tried to hide him from my ex-in-laws. Not that they didn't like him; just not for me.

The same night I met him; some one else was interested in knowing who I was. I was a new face to every body. One afternoon a man knocked at the door. I answer the door. He said his name was W.J. He pretended to be looking for some one who lived up the street from me. He pretended that he was at the wrong house. I told him where they lived; he talked for a while and left. The next day he came back and confessed. He said he had asked Mr. Dream who I was and decided to come by. W.J worked in another city. He had to go pass the subdivision where I lived every day. He would stop many nights after work. When it would snow; people could not get up on the hill where I lived; but some how W. J. would get up no matter how much snow was on the ground. When we met; I was divorced, and he was married. When he got divorced, I was married, I got divorced again; he was married. So we just remained friends through the years; more about him later.

The reason mother did not like the dream boy for me; she said he was a woman beater. She told me; "he was going to whip my draws in my <u>A.S&S AND PULL THEM OUT, AND WHIP THEM IN AGAIN</u>". After I started going out with Mr.D; I would be ill. I really thought I was ill. I visited the Doctor twice; trying to find out what was wrong. One day it downed on me: you are not ill; you are in love, and you are trying to hide it. After that I got free. I did not care who knew it. I was not ill any more. He was my <u>Dream</u> man. We would go out and have a ball. I was afraid to meet his family; first I met his Mom, and Dad; I met his two Sisters later. They all treated me very kindly. His Mother had a Sister; and she was sweet as could be. She was disabling; and was confined to the bed. We all hit it off very well. I would go over some days and talk to his Aunt. It did not make any difference that I had been married and had seven children by the way they treated me. Everybody called his Aunt Mama C. His mom worked well up in her eighties. She would hire reputable people to come in to take good care of her Sister.

21.
Divorcing Jahari, Marring Mr. D

Two years later I got my divorce from Jahari. Dream Boy would spend the night some times. I would hire a baby sitter, and we would go out every week end and dance. I would do my friends hair to make enough money to take us out and buy our drinks. I never used my kid's money for any pleasure. I allowed him to move in. I was not raised to shack; and I was raising my children to be respectable beings. We went to another town and got married in the Court House. His best friend was our witness. Every thing was great for a while. Then he began to change.

Mr.D began to get jealous. When we were at the club; he said I was watching some guy across the way. And the fights started. I saw what my mother was seeing in him. We never get too old to listen to our parents. They have lived it. They can see much father than we can.

If he said; "I'm going to beat your m.f.a; I could look for it". Every body loved hitting me on my head. We were at his Mother; Mama Sweet's house one day standing on the steps talking; Dream Boy slapped me in her presence; she got so angry with him. She blessed him out. She and I had a great relationship. She treated me as her Daughter too. She had three daughters including me. His Father died a few months after we got married.

The Attorney who filed for my divorce was really up in age. But he was still practicing Law. He did my divorce at an affordable price for me. He was in his late seventies and still practicing. He took care of all my Legal Business at a discount. Every Thanksgiving and Christmas he would meet me at the Grocery Store; and fill my basket with what ever groceries I needed to make dinner for my kids. He commended me for being so brave to stick with my Children at such young age. I could have left too. He said; that is why he helped us. He was an old white man sweet on a young black woman. He needed me to stop by the office every once and a while to make him feel good. He practiced law on over into his late eighties. He was my friend when I needed Legal assistance. After he was unable to come into the City, I would have to go into the Country to his house to get my files. He introduced me to his sweet little wife. I didn't know he had died until I saw it in the paper. He once was a very prominent attorney.

TAKING IN MR.D'S KIDS

Mr.D had two kids by his ex- girl friend. When she found out we were married; she brought the children and left them on the porch. We took them in as our own and loved them. He got a job at a Steel plant. After working there a few months, he got fired. I went to the manager and talk to him, I looked him in the eye and explain to him that we had nine children; and would he please reconsider re-hiring Mr. D, so he did. I was working at a Department store which was newly open up in the city. I worked there a few months. Some times I was scheduled to work till closing. I lived miles away. Sometimes I did not know how I was going to get home. One winter night after getting off work; the wind chill was thirty five miles an hour; and the chill factor was well below zero. I discovered the car I was using that night was out of gas. I took the gas can from the trunk and walked to the gas station and purchased gas. While transferring the gas to the vehicle; I spilled some on my hands. My hands became frost bitten. By the time I arrived at my house; I was in so much pain; it even hurt to cry. It took hours to stop the pain. I always heard that if your hands or feet are frost bitten; just soak them in cold water, it did not work that time. Gas has a different effect than water if it gets on your hands when the weather is cold.

I really like helping the elderly. I had heard that there was an opening at a nursing home; and they were hiring. I went and got an application. I applied for the job, and was hired. I took the bus every day. The bus stop was two and a half miles from my house. One of the ladies who worked there; was a member of the same church I attended. She became concerned for me having to get the bus to work; mainly because of the distance I lived from the bus stop. She directed me to an Auto Dealer whom she knew very well. She said; 'tell him Rosie sent you". My credit was very bad and I did not have anything in my name. I talked to him for months trying to convince him that I could be trusted. Every few days, I was at the Dealership talking to that Manager. Finally he said; "I am going to trust you with this car, and I am holding you accountable; not your husband; you only". He was convinced that I was not giving up.

I was so happy. That was my first owned auto in my name. It was a canary yellow Nash Rambler station wagon. I had an auto large enough for my family. The kids were so excited. We would have our own transportation to go to the laundry mat, Church, grocery store, and give them a ride to school those cold mornings. Mr. D quit the Steel plant and took a job at another Factory, which was about ninety miles round trip. He needed transportation; so I let him drive the Rambler. That job paid more money. He drove it every day, and never checks the oil, and burned the engine up. We did not have the money for a new engine and he quit the job because he said he had no way to get there. I had to pay for a car that I did not have. But I never missed a payment. Dream Boy decided to breake into a printing shop where they print checks. I was so surprised; when the police came to arrest him. I wanted to tell the police you have the wrong man, because he has never been into any trouble before. He was arrested and released on his on accordance and later paid a fine. His Family could not believe it either. I never have had good credit. As earnest as I am and do pay my bills on time. I am a woman of my word. I have always met men who don't have good credit. I have suffered all my adult life for the like of good credit; because of some one else.

The kids had a baby kitten. It had just been weaned from its mom. They trained it to do so many tricks. It was their heart. I had never cared for cats, because I had no idea they could be trained. I had fallen in love with the kitten too. Jebez said the girls always ganged up on him, so he got back at them by covering up the litter box with some clothes so the cat would use them instead of her box. He knew that would make me angry and take the kitten away. When she did, we had no way of knowing why she went on the clothes. Once you show a cat where her litter box is, that is where they always go. Instead of me handling the situation; Mr. D took the cat away. That caused a bad feeling with the kids against him. They begged for a second chance. I even tried to talk him out of it. It seemed he got a kick out of taking her away because they loved that cat. I didn't want the cat to be taken away either. She was smart! We did not know Jebez set it up; until years later. He told us the truth when he got grown. He knew he would have gotten a whipping. He got a kick from seeing the girls crying and begging.

Mr. D and I went to the grocery store one evening; and when we returned; his kids were gone. Their mother had come and taken them away. We really did miss them. They had been with us over a year; we loved having them. I never saw them again. Mr. D did not know anything about disciplining any kids. I always took care of that; even with his kids. They had never lived with him before. He was painting the ceiling; one day; and I was reprimanding my number six child Rae about something she had done; and he hit her in the mouth with the paint brush. The bush was full of paint. We almost broke up over that incident. To me that was abuse. No one was going to abuse my kids if I knew about it. I was like a mother hen over her biddies with my children. We were very close knit. We talked about everything when they were growing up. I was not over protective; I just knew children should be reprimanded with love. I always stayed away from the kind of treatment I endured while growing up. I would; whip those back-ends, but with a switch when needed. I whipped Maggie one time when she was fifteen with an extension cord. I had a hard time forgiving myself for that, because it was about what a grown up said she did. It turned out not to be true.

THE BREAK UP WITH MR. D

One evening we had been out at the club; when we came home and had gone to bed. Some time during the night Mr. D had gone into the kid's room; and was after Louise. That next morning while I was getting ready for work; she told me that he had come to her bed. I did not have time to address the issue at that time. I took her to work with me. She did not want to stay at home. When I got off work that evening; we had a discussion about it; and I asked him to move out. He did leave.

After we had been separated about four months; my two Buddies and I were out at the Legion on a Saturday night. When the Band had their intermission; one of the musicians asks me to walk out to his Van with him to get another instrument. We stood out side and talked for a minute. Mr.D had one of his buddies watching me.

When I came in and sat down at the table where my Buddies were; he walked up to our table and insists that I go out side. I got up because I did not want my reputation to get tainted by a scene in public. Every body looked up to me. I was a public figure in the community. So I politely got up, and while I was walking; I was looking for a bottle on some one's table, because I knew it was going to be a fight. No body had a bottle on their table, only glasses. I was wearing eye glasses for fashion. As we got out side he hit me and knocked my glasses off; and I went into him. By then the Ladies I was with had come out side too. One was yelling beat his ass. I was really fighting back. It seems that everybody I met wanted to beat me up. I decided its time to stop crying and fight back. He could see he was not winning; so he cut me with a razor. He was aiming for my face; but I was heating him up with all I had. I think I shocked him. If I had not had on the type of dress I was wearing; he really would have cut me bad. The dress was made of shells; and the razor was dull. The razor caught up in that shell which protected me from what really could have been a disaster. Both my girl friends took me to the hospital and I received twenty six stitches on my thigh and arm. The hospital reported the incident to the authorities and Mr. D was arrested.

22.
A New Job

MOTHER CAME BACK

SIX WEEKS LATER BIG Sis told me they were hiring at the Electric Company; where she was working. The job would have paid enough for me to get off Welfare. I was still healing from the razor wounds. I asked my Mother to come and be with the children so I could get the job. Since Dream Boy was gone out of the house she was willing to come back to help out. I was hired at the Company; but it was against the company's policy to be hired if you had any abrasions or lacerations. I lied and said I had none. I was blessed to have a relative who was a foreman in the department that every one must start out in before being placed out on the floor. He gave me light duty for six weeks. Then I was placed out on the floor. The job paid more money than I had ever received on any job.

Another young lady and I car pooled with a man who worked at the Plant. He was from Trinidad. He drove here in America the way they drive over there. He drove a small car, and dotted in and out of traffic. A Transfer Truck did not mean a thing to him. He took all kind of chances. By the time we reach the job; I would be so nervous I could hardly do my job; which was soldering wires to a fuse on an assemble line. We had to catch every other unit and solder two wires as the line continue rolling. A lot of people from our City were employed there. Jahari was remarried and he was also employed there. Big sis had been employed there a while. I asked her to co-sign on a loan for me there at the credit union. I had not been on the job long enough to get the loan on my own signature. I thought that would be a start to build up my credit. I planed to be employed there as long as necessary.

I was only able to work six months. My mother was physical ill when she came back to be with the children. I had one more payment to make on the loan which meant that the last payment would come out of my last check. Big Sis loud talked me all over the area where I was working in my department. She was making every one think that I was leaving her to pay my loan. One lady said; "I thought you said that you and she had been friends for fifteen years" I said we have; "she said if she is your friend I wouldn't want any enemies". The loan was paid and I quit work to take care of my mother.

But big sis really was my friend. If it had not been for her many times I don't know what we would have done. She saw to me getting to the laundry matt, grocery store or where ever I or the kids had a need to go. She even tried to persuade me not get a divorce from Jahari. She was never in favor of any divorcing. There were times I used her car to go to the clubs. It would be so lonely on that hill where we lived some week-ends. She hated to see me quit the job, because she knew that was a good job for me; and I needed the money. She was tired of seeing me struggling. She loved me as a sister; and what ever decisions I made would affect her because she looked out for us.

Mother Had Cancer

I knew my mother was ill. Lying around was not her thing. She stayed in bed a lot. I could not get her to agree to go to the doctor at first. She was afraid of surgery. One day at work, I heard a voice so loud; it spoke to me so plain, it said; your Mom has cancer. I looked around to see who said it. I finally convinced her to go to a doctor. When he finished examining her; he took me in another room, and told me his diagnoses. She did have cervical cancer. The doctor said she needed surgery. She never asked me one time what the doctor said to me. She already knew. When we tried to contact her Insurance Co; so she could have the surgery. She had been paying into that Company for years. We found there was no such Company. She had been paying into what she thought was a Health plan, it was a fraud. The doctor gave her six months to live. He would not do the surgery because there was no money. He was a Gynecologist who had done Surgery on almost every woman in that City. Mother had not lived in the state long enough to get help from them. She lived much longer than six months; but she really was in lots of pain. The length of time she lived; the surgery probably would have saved her life.

The children had a long way to walk to school. We had very cold winters back in the 60s. It was hard to keep Ann with gloves. Glo and Maggie would take their gloves off and give to her She is the baby girl. Big sis would take them to school and pick them up for me. The kids needed under shirts. I did not have money to purchase them. I had met Mr.G. He contacted the Township Office and sent me to get a voucher for some warm undershirts for the kids. He knew the Supervisor personally, so they hooked me up with new under shirts for every body. I was still learning that you don't get something for nothing. That favor cost me a few dates. He wasn't a bad guy, he liked having fun. I knew that he drank sociality, but one night he got drunk and hit me. That was the end of that relationship. He tried to apologize; and tried everything to make it right; but it was over. I was tired of being hit.

My greatest nightmare was when I woke-up one day and realization had set in; and I said, girl—you have a great responsibility to deal with. I ask God to teach me how to raise these kids because; by then the oldest son, his grandma called him Pinny was getting into trouble big time. I was changing schools thinking it might be the teachers, but soon found out it was him. He and big sis's son would get into so much mischief together. Sometimes they would take the blame for things each other would do. Their thing was you don't snitch on each other. That went on until I changed schools, because I thought the teachers were picking on him. Then he met other kids to get into trouble with. I soon found out that it was really my child. He met another kid. They started robbing stores, out all hours of the night. Sometimes he did not come home at all. I had no help. Jahari had brothers who lived near by; but no one would help. I would tie him to the bed for punishment. He would go under the bed and go to sleep: because he would be so tired he was glade to be tied down; so it really was not punishment. No matter what I did to him; he didn't listen. These are the days they would call tying him to the bed child abuse.

Pinny came home one day after being away for a day; I fell down cross the bed and I cried so hard; he fell on me crying too; and begging mama don't cry, **I aint go do it no mo.** As soon as the tears were dry he was at it again. When his Dad was home he got whipping for a lot of things he did not do. He also got lots of whippings when he was very young; so he got tough. He got more whippings than love. One of his principals would always be at our house telling his dad things the child supposes to have done. There are always two sides to a story; your side; his side; and the truth. Grown ups will lie too. Jahari would whip him without hearing his side of the story. Pinny, Jebez and some of their cousins went to the park; they all jumped into the pool. Jebez jumped in and knew he could not swim and almost drowns. They pull him out just in time. When they got home, his cousin told Jahari what happened; Pinny got whipped so bad that Jebez cried for his brother. It was not his fault. Jebez knew he could not swim; but he jumped in anyway. I think he was glad his dad was gone. He never took time with the children. Pinny also knew there would be no male to discipline him. Even though they say I could whip like a man. Male children need their father in their lives. God never told a female to raise a son. Usually when males turn out to be great men under a female's hand; is because he- made up in his mind, that he wants to be great, and he wants to look out for his mom. My son was a follower. He followed the wrong crowd

After Jahari left; at age twelve, Pinny started running around with other kids getting into trouble. I would have to go to court so much; the police and most of the judges knew me. Sometimes I would stand outside the court room when the Judge called for a break; some of the Officers would come and talk to me as if they felt my pain. One time I had to get on the stand and tell the judge about my life on my son's behalf. I cried so; the States attorney was wiping his eyes trying to keep me from seeing him. They would let my son go. I saw that he was taking advantage of that; I had to stop defending him. He began to think; my mama can get me out of trouble.

Pinny was walking home from School one afternoon a Huge German Shepard befriends him and follows him home. He was the biggest and tallest dog we ever saw. We never knew where he came from. We advertised to see if any one would claim him, nobody did. The kids called him Duke. He was a great watch dog. He protected our house because there were no male around to protect us. If I spanked the kids I would have to put him out. Pinny and Duke went to the school play ground to play after school; and the dog saw the Principal; Pinny had a hard time holding the dog off of him. He said my son sic the dog on him. Pinny said he didn't; dogs can sense evil. The dog knew that the principal did not like Penny. He said the dog started growling as soon as he saw the Principal. We kept Duke three years. The same way he came is the same way he left. We had not ever seen a dog like him before. We have never seen another. We called him our Angel, sent to protect us

When Pinny was twelve he was sentence to a Penal Youth Farm for robbery. I thought my heart would burst out of my chest that cold day as I left the Court House. The wind was blowing. It was a below zero day. I didn't feel a thing. I HAD LOST CONTROLL OF MY SON. He was in and out of Youth Centers all through his youth. I had to depend on the goodness of people to take me to see him. I did not have transportation. A good friend name Al would take me and Glo to see him. We went regular to visit him. He would be in the hole some times when we get to the Center. He said they would put him in the hole naked; on a muddy cold ground for days; but for some reason he continued to get into trouble. Glo stood with me; she was always the one to go with me to visit him.

LOOSING OUR HOUSE

We were losing our house for taxes, and we had to move. I had heard about a Pastor who could help us get into one of the Projects down town. I went to see him. I knew we were doomed if we moved into the Projects around the corner from where we lived. Crime was already at its highest peek there. He was more than willing to help because I was going to have to pay a price for his services; but not with money. I did not know that then. He waited until we were in the middle of the transaction. No matter who I went to and ask for help; I had to pay a price. Whether he was the Doctor, Lawyer, Police, Employee or Pastor, there was a price I had to pay. To sum it all up; it was prostitution; so let's not fool ourselves; any time anything is paid for with sex; that is called prostitution. We categorize sin; but God don't. To Him all sin is as great as another. That's what I cooperated with to benefit my family. When we were young we were taught that you could get anything from a man with your body. As I look back over my life and realized what molestation does to children. I think it had affected me, because I was very permissive after my divorce. Not that I wanted to be, but My Dad was the first person to caress my breast. It felt unusual, and maybe good, but I knew it was something wrong with that picture. He was my father, and supposes to be protecting me. I always wondered why I had to pay such a price. I never presented myself in that manner. I never thought of myself as being attractive. I just needed help. I didn't want to do those things. Every time I would go to some one for help; I really needed it. They took advantage of me. Who; could need more help from them than a young green mother needing help for her children? When I began to understand molestation and how it affects one, I prayed for deliverance and God set me free because I was serious. He knew my heart. One person said to me; it seems as if I am blaming myself for the things that has happen to me. I think we go through things in order to be able to help some one else. I know I am not the only female who has been through these types of circumstances. I'm not blaming myself; I'm not blaming any one; this is my life. Today I don't think men even notice me. That is ok because now I am a whole person. I wonder sometimes if my husband notices me. You have to come to know who God say you are and be that person.

This Pastor kept his promise and pulled the necessary strings to get us moved in. It was a challenge because we lived out of the District; we weren't eligible to move in that district. My mother-in-law; Mama Sweet would let all of us come down to her house Monday through Friday; after school and stay until bedtime. We needed to use an address in that District in case anybody came by checking for our address. She did not want to see us set out without having a place to go; and she and I were very close. I could not tell her about the debt I had to pay to get that help. She knew that Pastor and looked up to him and respected him as a Pastor. This also, caused my mother and Mama Sweet to meet each other. They became friends because she had to come down to her house with us.

It took about six weeks for everything to become finalized for us to move in. When we got those keys we all were so happy. That meant we had running hot and cold water, bath tub, shower, a toilet we could flush, closets, and plenty sleeping space. I was working at the Hospital then. Even though my mom was ill, she packed most of the clothes, and shook every peace to get rid of the bugs. They were all in the walls. We could hear them crawling in the paneling. We did not bring one of those critters with us, and we never saw another one. It was such a blessing to be living in a home large enough to accommodate my family. The house we moved from had burned down before we realized we had left clothes in the attic. Lots of the kid's winter clothes were left in that attic. That is where we would store seasonal clothes because we had no closets. My mother still called my oldest son Pinny but he changed his name to Mickey. She didn't care what every body else called him; to her he was Pinny. I will call him Mickey.

At fourteen Mickey was released from the Farm. After we got settled in; I went back to school to get my eight grade diploma. I also tested to get my high school diploma; but I could not pass the Math and Comprehension part. My problem is because they just go over a review in order for us to pass the test. I quit school in fifth grade; review would not help me; I never had any part of high School classes. I really need to be taught as in school. To me review means; you have gone over it before. When I pass the eight grade exam; the teachers were Nuns; and they taught the class; not review.

My mother started to talk to me about going to see about my dad. She felt he was ill. She could feel things. If she told me something, it always did come to pass. There was an old saying when I was a kid: (if I tell you a hen dip snuff") "LOOK UNDER THE WING; AND THERE IS THE BOX". I called my sister; she confirmed that dad was very ill. I asked why she had not let me know, she never told me why. My dad was still my heart. I had not seen him in about five years. I could not go to visit him with all the children. I didn't own a car, or the finances. We would have had to stay in a hotel. Blacks could not stay in hotels in the South back then.

My mother kept the children, and I got the train and went down. When I arrived; my sister and I took a gentleman that she knew to help us bring our dad from that same two room Ark, where he was still living, when I was living at home. He could not walk. He was so light; the man lifted him by himself. We took him to my sister's house. I stayed two weeks to help out. At the hospital where I worked; I was a nurse's assistant, so I knew how to give him his baths. We put him in the hospital before I left; He said to me; "I did not kill that man that I was accused of killing". He made his piece; and in two weeks he was gone.

My mother was still hanging in there. Mama Sweet had hired her to take care of her sister who was an invalid. While she still worked. She refused to put her in a home. Mama Sweet took care of her until she died.

My brother borrowed his friend's auto and drove from the City to pick me up from where I lived. We drive back South for our dad's funeral. We stayed and helped haul tons of iron and steel out of my dad's Unit. All he had was one little corner for his bed. People would bring food to him. When he finishes eating he would set the plate beside the bed where he lay, because he was bed ridden. The rats would be after that food my dad could not eat. He would keep his rifle beside his bed and shoot the rats. He still had good eye sight. We sold the iron by the tons. Dad had a little TV. We never had a chance to ask him whether it was paid for. So I brought it back to Illinois with me; thinking it might be paid for. A few months later a Salesman from the Store knocked on my door asking about the TV. Of course I did not need it; I thought: just having something from my dad would be nice. I gave it back. He loved his young women, but when he got ill they were no where to be found.

On our way back after the funeral the car my brother had borrowed; had no working speed odometer. It was my turn to drive. As I come down off a hill there set the Police. He gave me a nice fat ticket. It was a long while before I saw my brother after that. When ever I'd see him; I would always be the one to find him. He was married to a very nice lady. She had several Children before they met; then they had children together. I would track my brother down whenever too much time passed by without hearing from him. He had so many of my dad's features. I met his wife and family, we bonded together. My children and I went to spend a week end with them once and he tried to seduce me. We were all sleeping on pallets on the floor, and he came crawling on the floor after he thought every one was sleeping. I was so hurt and shocked. He was my only brother; why would he want to do such a thing to his little sister. I never could be comfortable around him after that; but I still loved him. I lost contact with him. He had started to drink. He had contracted arthritis very bad while in the Army; and he had, had a hip replacement. Some how I found out he was in the hospital; and we went to see him. He had separated from that wife and married again. They had moved to Cairo IL. He brought her around a few times. After they parted he moved to Mound City that's where he died in his sleep. His buddies said he had lain down to take a nap and did not wake up. I don't know what happened to her. She was on Oxygen and was not able to attend his funeral. She would not have been able to stand that heat anyway. That is the hottest little town I ever been to. It sets way down in a valley. It's very damp and steaming hot. We almost cooked while at the funeral. My niece who lives in St-Louis notified me of his death. I guess the people who live in Cairo are use to the heat there.

23.
Mother's Death

MICKEY TOOK HER DEATH HARD

AFTER WE MOVED DOWN town Mickey had gotten into more trouble at age fourteen; and the Police came to arrest him; Mickey ran out the back door and jumped into the Police car and took off. When they apprehended him they arrested him. He got probation for that incident. When he was seventeen he went back to Prison. Mickey was my Mother's heart. He had committed another robbery, and had been incarcerated all most a year before coming to trial. When the trial started, it lasted two weeks. I attended every day. The trial ended on a Friday. He was sentence to five years. I had learned to guard my heart and not let Mickey cause me to have a break down. My Mom worked that day, as she walked through the door, she asks; with anticipation; where is Pinny? I said he didn't make it out this time. She went up stairs; went to bed, stop eating. She was grieving and the cancer was getting worse.

One night Jebez and I were sitting down stairs, watching T.V.; we heard this loud clomp. He hit about two steps to her room; mother was trying to go out of the window. We called the Ambulance. Thank God Jebez was home. He hung around home a lot. He is a mama's boy too, but he is not lazy. Because mom had been in a mental hospital before, her case worker ordered us to take her there. They thought she'd had another break-down. The hospital only kept her for a few days. The

117

Doctors said it was the cancer that had affected her blood vessels. That caused the confusion. The cancer had taken its toll. All she would do was bath as many times a day as necessary and eat Anacin tablets for pain. She never got too ill to keep her own body clean

She really feared hospitals. I finally convinced her to go, by explaining to her that her diet would be better for her there. She finally agreed to go one week before Thanksgiving. I was there every day after work I was with her all day Thanksgiving Day. She looked well and she kept telling me; Mama's going to be all right. Friday morning after thanksgiving at 2:A.M; I got the call; by the time I reached the hospital, she had expired. I did not get there in time to say good-by. She was only fifty five. She lived two years after the doctor gave her six months. She would tell her sisters; if kind treatments would keep her from dying; she would never die. I was kind to my mother. I did all I could for her. I loved my mother very much. I really miss her. She could make me laugh telling jokes. She was very active. Even after she got ill; she cooked every day and changed the furniture around sometimes.

One day when the kids got home from school; she had moved the couch. They didn't like the way it looked. Louse asked; grandma; did you move the couch? She asks three times before mother answered; when she did answer; she said; "kiss that couch's ass. We laughed so-- hard. We still do. We still talk about her and some of the funny things she did. Most of the children were not born when she was so mean and the ones who were born were too small to remember. She had calmed down long enough that we were able to enjoy each other.

Mother wanted to be buried back in the South. She always reminded me not to bury her in Illinois. We waked her body here where she attended church. She had some friends there too. The Sweet-Heart of our club had become a good friend to us. We had been friends since club days. He had heard about me through some fellows that worked at the Yard before he became the Sweet-Heart of our Social Club. The guys at the Yard would talk about the young lady with seven children, and that I was a great mother to be so young. So he set out to meet me. We became very good friends I was at his house with another couple when I got the call from the hospital about my mother's breathing. He had met her before. I had told him about my mother's wishes. I would not have been able to take my family down South for her funeral; and

I did not have anyone to leave them with either. Mr. Turner drove my children all the way to Mississippi; and paid for my mother's body to ride on the train; and paid for Ann and me to ride with her body. That was three whole fairs because Ann was fourteen. My Mother had her burial policy down South at their family Funeral Home. She was put away beautiful; just the way she wanted. Thanks to Mr. Turner.

When Glo and I went to see Mickey; and told him that grandma was gone. He cried so hard and said; "I killed my grandma". Mickey's life has been a roller coaster; he has been cut, stabbed, shot, in shoot outs, automobile accidents, broken leg, and homeless. Those were all he would tell me about. He said he would never tell me all the things that have happen to him. He was shot with a thirty eight. The bullet enlarged in his bottom lip. At the emergency room, the Doctor said; this was a first time for them to see a 38 bullet enlarge it self in a lip. Mickey's lips are very thin. He said he was sitting in a car, waiting on a dude; he heard a noise; as he turned to see what he heard; he was shot in the lip.

My Sister's Death

I had surgery to remove a tumor that I had been carrying since being pregnant with my sixth child. It had grown to the size of a grape fruit. I had almost recovered from the surgery when I received a call that my sister had had a stroke. She fell and hit her head on the corner of her bed; and suffered a coma and died. I was she had high blood pressure, and she had drank a beer, they think that might have elevated the pressure and caused her to fall.

Her husband and she had just begun their lives after him coming home from the penitentiary. Their children were grown and gone. They were free again. He had served time for murder at that same place where my daddy and uncle had served.

One day a neighbor being nosie; called him at work, and told him that the man my sister was seeing was parked in front of his house. Persey left his job in a rage; went home and shot the man with a shot gun, and killed him. He served five years in prison for that crime.

I had lost my dad, my mom, and my sister within one year. Mr.D said he had compassion and felt that I needed him back to lean on. He went on to say that's too much trauma for one person to stand along.

119

He assured me I needed him. We got back together. He said; "after everything you've been through; you need some-one to comfort and help you through these times". I was so gullible to think he might have changed. A few months after we got back together I caught him coming out of a rooming house with another woman. We argued, he lied and we put it behind us.

I told him a couple of my co-workers and I was going to a movie after work. He said ok; since it was still early when the movie ended; we decided to stop in the club to have a beer. I got home about nine o'clock. He started an argument, and the results of it turned into a fight. The kids were up stairs listening. Glo took a shoe and beat on the floor above us to get his attention. That stopped the fight. She had told Mickey about him cutting me with the razor incident when she and I went to the prison to visit him. He was still angry about that; but he had said if I was happy with the guy he would not interfere. When this fight happened, Mickey was home from prison, the kids told him what had happen. He said time out: he needs to feel what it feels like to get your butt kicked. Mickey and one of his friends waited for my husband that night; but he did not come home. That was the first time he had ever stayed out all night. I knew then it was time for me to get out before some one was hurt or dead.

We separated again; .this time I got a divorce. I was still getting assistance from the State; because, He wasn't my children's father.

GOING TO BEAUTY SCHOOL

I was determined to be a stay home mom. I had lost one child to the system I was determined that I would not loose another one. I had had several case workers, within the last five years; and had inquired about Beauty School from all of them. That was what I wanted to do so I could work at home and be with my children. Each case worker said there was no way they could help me; and that they knew of no such programs.

Then I got a break; I was signed to a male case worker, and I was still trying to find a way to get into Beauty School. I asked him about the opportunity to go; he said; we don't send anyone, but I can make arrangements for you to go through what we call MAN-POWER. I was so happy; the time was right. I had to go to the Employment Service to enroll. The Agents were not in agreement with the School I wanted to enroll into. When I told the Agents what School I wanted to enroll into; he was furious.

It was an all white School. My friend owned a Beauty School, and the Agent could not under-stand why I would not want to go there. We went round and around until he really saw that he could not change my mind. His co-worker; said to him; "let her go where she want to go". My dream was to have a chain of integrated Beauty Salons around the Country. Not that I couldn't have had that under my friend. I felt our friendship would have hindered my progress. I have a problem comprehending. I knew we would be talking about more personal things than teaching and studying. I needed one on one attention. I was over whammed about going to the school I chose.

The Manager did not want me to come there. He called my friend and told her that; A COLORED GIRL had enrolled into his Beauty School; and that she should call me to see if she could change my mind. The way he pronounced my last name; she thought she did not know who the girl was. So she called; when I answered the phone; she said hello Mrs. Evans (she mispronounced my name) I recognized her voice immediately. I said; hello this is Mag. That's what all my friends called me. When we moved from her neighborhood we lost touch. She did not know my married name; and after she got over the surprise of who I was; she said; "I can talk to you candidly". She said; "I received a call from this Beauty School and they don't want you to go to go there". I said to her that is all the more reason I want to go. We talked; I explained why I needed to go there. I let her know it was nothing against her.

I found out later it was not the Owner who called. When he found out what had happen; he fired that Manager. That could have caused him a law suit. Everything went great after that. I got lots of help through my teachers. They spent much of their time helping me with my studies. It wasn't easy because I only had a fifth grade education. Maggie stuck with me. She was in Collage and could help me brake down those words. Some times she would fall a sleep. I would wake her up crying; because that theory was hard; but the practical was very easy. I could style hair before going to school; but the theory was collage material. The Clients would be waiting in line to request me as their operator. The shampoo area was in view of the students styling area. When the shampoo seats were filled, the clients could watch us style other clients at our stations. I won first place in a beauty contest that our school held the first three months. Louise was my model. The Owner made it clear; that I was there to work toward getting my license not to make money for him, and I should spend as much time studying as needed.

I can say that was the hardest task I had ever taken on, except raising my children alone. We had to learn the Anatomy of the head and Muscles and take many exams. Our teachers taught us everything it took to be a good Cosmetologist. We had to have thirty five hours of business. Each student had to work the cash registers and greet the customers. Greeting the customers is so important. You have to make them feel that you are glad that they your Customers; and that you appreciate them. I gain so much favor with my Teachers. I got all the help I needed from them.

Maggie helped me all the way. My friend Mr. Turner would let me use his car for my transportation to school during the week. Over in the semester a young white Student enrolled in the School. He saw that I was struggling with the tests. He told his uncle that I was having trouble taking our weekly tests. His uncle was a Forman at one of the near by factories. He told his nephew that he would be willing to come to my house which was in the Projects and help me. He and his uncle would come to my house and teach me how to study for a test. The problem was I did not know how to study; to take a test. I had gained three great friends at the school. They were having trouble too, they joined us. All of us would meet at my house. We made a social event out of it. We started to meet from house to house getting prepared. After learning how to study; I had no more problems taking the tests; which got me ready for the State test. Our teachers had warned us about the red headed examiner at the State Board; who would take points off students if they drop their combs. I was a comb dropper at school; but I did not drop one comb at the State. Most students only had a one day exam. Mine was a two day exam. Mr. Turner took me both days. I was so nervous; that he had to stop the car so I could regurgitate. Both days were below zero weather. I passed the exam with flying colors. We had to wait six weeks to find out if we passed. That was the longest six weeks ever. One of those Ladies and I are still keeping in touch with each other and are very good friends We have told our children to make sure they get in touch with which ever one of us leave first. We try to get together once a year. The Other two Ladies are deceased. I don't know what happen to the nephew and uncle.

At that School; each student would be placed in a Salon upon graduation. I was placed in an up-scale Department Store that housed an exclusive Beauty Salon; at the Boston Store. I worked a year; and I started having trouble with my hand, like loosing feelings in my left hand. We did a lot of back combing (TEASING). Before the store closed; I went to work at Mr. Turner's Sister's Beauty Shop. I worked with them about a year. I decided I wanted to go work with my friend Big Sis at House of Beauty. Big Sis had also become a Cosmetologist. She graduated from our friend's School. She never let me do anything that she didn't do. I worked there a while and from there to another Shop the Comb. I made the mistake of telling the customers, I was leaving the Boston Store before telling the manager. The Manager was at store number two when the customers called her crying about me leaving. The Manager had to leave the store to come to see what all the commotion was about.

She asks if I was leaving the Salon. I said I was; she said she wished I had told her first. I had changed so many ladies lives by building their confidence. One lady in particular, I had convinced her to get a hair cut and a high lightener in her hair. It did wonders for her. That changed her life to the point of her being ask out on dates. Before the change she looked much older than her years, and never got asked out. I hated to leave them. Caucasians were getting a lot of teasing back then but the teasing was too much stress on my hands. Later both stores closed.

I met Santa Clause while working at; one of the Salons I never wanted to get involved with him because he was married. But every day he was by that shop. He showed me every reason why I needed him to help me. He was working two jobs; as a contractor, and a grocery store. He had worked at the store five years; and in charge of closing the store after hours. He was the janitor there .They found out he was steeling meat; he was bringing it to me for my babies. I had no idea he was steeling it. I knew he worked there. He said he really did not need the second job, and he had not thought about stealing before. I felt bad about it. I was honest with him and there were no romantic feelings involved. He knew the truth, but he continued to help me. He always had plenty of money because he was a glass contractor over the entire City.

After I graduated; I was able to become self supported and discontinue help from the State. I never got the chance to open the chain of Salons, but I purchased a house and added an extension on the end of it; and open my own Salon five years later. Some of the Beauticians from other Beauty shops joined us and attend Conventions, and Seminars every year; from State to State, and all through the years. A bunch of us attended one of the largest Universities for a week. We also united with the National Beauty Culture League. Three of us, received our B.A. in Cosmetology in Philadelphia, Pa, under that League. I studied Poise and Charm classes for two years. We kept up with the trend.

The Owners and operators of that shop helped every one in need. We all worked together well and had lots of fun. Big sis also came to work there with us. We looked forward to coming to work. I was always telling jokes. We were determined not to have a gossiping Salon. So one of the Owners and I entertained the customers. If you were a Cosmetologists; and needed a place to work; you could always go to that Beauty Shop for help. Twice I moved away from the City, and when I returned I would need a place to work. They would be kind enough to let me rent a booth, and I could set my own price until I build my clientele .As soon as word would get around that I was back, my clientele would all come back, then I would pay what every one else paid for my booth. One of the owners and I have always been like sisters. I guess I never stop looking for that sister relationship. If she could take her heart out and keep on living; she would give it to you. I call her husband my brother. We like to debate with each other. My jokes partner became ill and left us. She was greatly missed. One of her daughters' ask me to be her mentor, I was honored.

24.
Meeting WT

THE YEAR AFTER I graduated from Cosmetology school; I met the man of my life. He was a twenty year Career Soldier. Louise worked at the ammunition plant where he was stationed. She invited him over meet her mother without me knowing about it. He had promised her he would, months by. She said she had given up on him ever coming by. I really didn't want to meet any one. I had been through so-- much hurt. I really didn't want any more romantic relationships.

One Sunday afternoon WT came by. I was up stairs watching TV. My daughter called to me; mama-- there is some one who wants to meet you. I ask; who is it-- She said come down. I said; I don't want to meet who ever it is. I decided to come down, here stand this tall handsome man looking up at me. I thought to myself; I know he is up to no good. I was a little cold to him, but I warmed up because my Mom always said; be kind to people in your home. He said he thought to himself; OH; she's hard; I like'um like that. He introduced himself; and I did the same. So I started calling him WT. He began coming by regular, pretty soon everyday. Two and three times a week he would pick me up from work and we would head for the Big City. We were having so much fun, it never dunned on me that I was footing the bill. He had already served one year in Vietnam before I met him, and had signed up before he met me to return back for another year, after getting there he decided to do eighteen months. We were friends eight months before he lift. He left his new automobile with me. I was horned that he would trust me enough to leave his automobile. It was so sharp. It was a yellow and black Ski Lark; I took very good care of it. I didn't ride any males in it; and I kept it maintained.

After divorcing Mr. D, he always would show up at the Clubs where I was. There were six different clubs that we all hung out at. No matter which one I'd choose; here comes my ex. I could not talk to any males. He would tell them I was his wife. One evening I was in the club; and he insisted that I go with him to his residence. I went with him; because he did not care where he created a scene. I begged him to leave me alone. As he was driving, and slowed down to turn the corner, I jumped out of the moving car. I landed on my butt. I was in so much pain, but he forced me to go with him anyway. He was living with his Sister. I was afraid to tell her what had happen. I had to spend the night with him. I had no way home. I think hitting that hard concrete is what started my back trouble. My spine was already out of line. I had already periodically visited the Chiropractic before meeting him while having the babies.

Another evening I was at the Legion and here comes my ex. He says he is going to mess up the car I was driving. I said to him; go right on. The man who own that automobile is in Vietnam; and he would not hesitate at all about treating you as one of those Viet Congs he is fighting over there. That will be common to him. That's what they do in Viet Nam. They are trained to kill.

I told him that I had purchased a knife; one that opens with a switch. All I have to do is touch a switch and it will open. I told him I am afraid of you. It is dangerous to bully people who fear you. I will probably be still cutting on you, after you are dead. That is what happens when one is afraid. They loose it for a period of time. He says to me; that make sense: I did not know you were afraid of me. That was the reality that stopped his harassing and bulling me.

MY TRIP TO CALIFORNIA

When WT got his orders to leave Vietnam; he called me and asks me if I would like to meet him in California. I was surprised and elated. I had never flown. As a matter of fact I had said that I would never fly because of fear. The fear left me when he called. So I started preparing. I made myself a beautiful white vinyl two piece cape pants suit, along with some other out-fits. The cape was flare with pants to match. The trip was two weeks away. I was so excited that I could not sleep. The day finally arrived. When I stepped on that Air plain; the first thing this handsome white guy said to me; "THAT IS A SHARP SUIT YOU ARE WEARING". He kept me company and that took away some of the fear. Plus all I could think about was seeing WT. He was already there waiting, when I arrived to met the plane with that big wide smile. We had a beautiful time in Monterey California. He had a buddy who had just come home from the Nam We spent time with him and his wife.

Big sis had asked if we would go to L. A. to check on her son who was in Prison there. We had to fly in a commuter plane there. They are scarier than the passenger planes; but for a friend, I had to do it. After we got there, we rented a car and drove up in the mountains. Our ears were popping; we were so high up. It took a while for them to clear up. Her son did not expect any visitors. We had a nice visit. I did not mind the trip. He is my favorite nephew. We spent the day with him and returned back to Monterey. We stayed one week there. Big sis was relieved to hear her son was well and had a positive attitude. He did not have much time to serve. The crime was not serious.

We were still living in the projects. WT spent more time at our house than at the Army Barracks. He would drive from the projects to his job We were parting hardy. What I really liked about WT; he was honest. He always told me that he wanted to get back with his wife. He was not divorced. I always loved honesty. He had signed up to be an Army Recruiter. In order to take the classes he had to go back to his home town. We talked every day. He called me one evening and said; He and his wife were getting back together. I was happy and sad all at the same time. I was happy he was doing what he so much wanted; but I was going to miss him.

I never let any grass grow under my feet. I began to see some one else after ten weeks. One evening my friend and I were sitting in the living room watching TV. There was a knock at the door. I opened it, it was WT. He was back. I was happy to see him. The friend knew it was over for us. He called a few t times and finally stopped. All of us enjoyed WT. The kids adored him. I had told my youngest daughter that WT and I were not getting married; she cried. He convinced Jebez to go into the Army because he had quit school. I had told him he must either go back to school or get a job; so he chooses the Army. He served three years; and helped me financially while he was there. WT was the male figure in their lives. He had graduated from recruiting; and was now working in the City along with some other Recruiters. He traveled there five miles five days a week to and from his job. He would reach his quota each month by enlisting young men into the Military. He never came short. It was challenging knocking on so many doors each day, but that's what he enjoyed until he retired from the military.

One morning about five o'clock there was a big explosion; rocks were flying everywhere. WT was sleeping in the nude. Maggie thought the war had come to America. She ran down stairs screaming. WT was out of bed trying to get into his pants. She rushed in our room and fell on her knees and hugged WT around his legs. She was screaming; they are here! They promised they wouldn't come! OH God they are here! She thought we were being bombed. She never realized that WT was in his birthday suit. After getting into his pants, he got her and everyone calm down and left for work, the kids left for school, and I went to the beauty shop to work. We found out from the news there had been a robbery at a gas station the thugs dropped the gas hose and which caused the gas to run into the sewer pipes and that's what caused the explosion.

Moving in with WT

WT decided to purchase a Condo near The City Where he would be closer to his job. I had just got a __BIG__ reduction on my rent. He came up with the idea that he wanted me to move in with him. I said no you are too wishey washy. He showed me all the reasons it would work. It was a nice three bed room Condo. All the kids were starting to leave home. The two younger girls were the only two still at home. I would have had to vacate the housing after all the children leave the house hold; I would no longer be eligible to live there. Jebez had served his three years in the Army. He was on his head to get married. I tried to talk him out of it at least for a while. He did not listen and got married. I told WT that the deduction in my rent would be of great help to me. If I moved in with him and he start acting crazy; I would not be able to go back to the projects. He assured me everything would be fine. I threatened that something un-pleasant will happen to him if he deceived me. I might even shoot him. Oh no he said; he promised everything will be fine. I gave up the projects and moved in with him. Things were good for a few months. School was still in session for a few more months. I made arrangement with Jebez and his wife for the two girls to stay with them until school was out.

Santa Clause was still around, and would do for me whatever I asked. Even though he did not want me to move, but to please me; he got the truck and paid for the move. I move in with WT. He could not even pay for me to move in with him. Managing money was not something he did very well. He got his pay once a month. Everything was great for a few months, almost a year. I continued working back in my home town at the Beauty Shop. I would drive back and forth five days a week about thirty five miles one way. Big Sis would come and spend some week-ends with us. We would take her bowling with us. We would go almost every week-end

WT started to act cold toward me. No talking, no loving, no explanation, or anything. I continued to cook, do laundry. Iron his uniform shirts, cleaning, and working. I would ask; what was wrong. Is it anything I did? After few weeks passed; he said his wife had called and wanted to come to the City to talk to him. I said ok! what's the big deal? Wait to see what she wants to talk about. He could not pay for a hotel for them to go; and she could not come to the house; because I was there; so he decided to go to her City; about four hours drive. He did not want her to know I lived with him. Our relationship was four years in the making. She knew he was seeing someone in that time frame. While he was gone I thought about the situation; I told myself; girl--you don't have to put up with this.

When Santa came by the shop; I told him what was going on, and I wanted to move back; but I did not have any place to move. I had been looking at some apartments. He said; "you don't want to move into no apartment" so he left the shop to look for a house for me. He found a house that same day; he came back to the shop and took me to see it. I fell in love with the house right away. He paid the security deposit, and paid for a truck along with some guys to go to move me out of WT'S Condo; to the house he found for me. The house was for rent with option to buy. It was a two bed room, living room and kitchen with a full crawl space for storage.

My Own HOUSE

When WT got back; and unlocked the door; all that condo had was an echo. I was gone. I rented the house with the option to buy it. The Land Lords had to sell because the husband had killed a man in self defense. The man who was killed; and the owner of the house; had had a fight earlier that day. The land lord was at home, thinking the argument had been settled. The other man could not let it go; so he busted in the Land Lord's house and was shot to death. It did not faze me that some one had died there. They needed to rent the house; and hopefully to sell the house; for monies to hire an attorney.

Within a year they were ready to sell; I was not ready. I did not have the down payment or the closing cost; some how at the closing my realtor showed; that I had the fifteen hundred dollars needed as the down payment. I do not know what he did, but the sellers did not find out until all the papers were signed. They were very up set; but it was too late. I didn't even have to be at the closing. I had purchased a house and did not know how I did it. I did not have any money saved yet to purchase it. His wife said her husband still got some time for the murder. I don't know how much. She and her son would stop in to visit some time. She began to drink a lot, and they stop coming by.

I did not have a refrigerator yet. Another neighbor came by and left a portable one on my porch. She said I could have it, she didn't need it. It was a blessing until I was able to purchase one; then I used it in the beauty shop for many years.

She would stop in and visit once in a while. She just needed some one to talk to. She told me she was moving; we lost touch. The house was on the near west side of the city. It was a very quite area. I was the only black in the neighbor hood. One night there was a knock on the door. There was a tavern one half blocks down the street. The guys had made a bet that one of then could seduce me. I told him off very intelligent; through the closed door. He went back to the bar; some how some one heard about the plot, and told me what the bet was. I did not have any more trouble. The old man across the street tried to act prejudice; but we became friends. He just needed some one to encourage him. That's what I did every chance I got. You don't have to fall into other people traps; just ask God what they need and how to provide it. Who is better to know what we need than the one who made us? If you buy a Chrysler, you wouldn't take it to a Buick dealer for repair. Take it to the one who made it. I moved to Away after again after we befriended each other, but he would still act a little with drawn. I was moved away nine months; when I moved back, I went over to see the old man; he said he missed me. I was shocked! That's when I figured out the word prejudice is a miss used Word. I had been warned by the neighbors that he was

Society describes prejudice as HATE; but it is a disposition more favorable to one thing, or person than to another. It's not hate; if it was hate; we would not want to be like each other. We copy from each other. I would not want to copy anything from anybody that I hated. When we come to except that Acts 17:29 said> "And He has made from one blood every nation of men to dwell on all the face of the earth, and has determined their preappointed times and boundaries of their habitations".

NEW KITCHEN

A friend of mine had her kitchen redone. She invited me to come see her beautiful kitchen cabinets an eighteen year old had built for her. She worked with his father at a Factory. They were beautiful. She gave me his phone number and I got in touch with him. That young man remodeled my kitchen for one thousand dollars. I had my sink set in the middle of the kitchen as an island with a large counter top all in one; and new cabinets on the walls. I also had him to build a breakfast nook around my bay windows. We encouraged him to go into business. I don't know if he did. He built them in the year of seventy five. When I sold the house in 2001 they were still like new. No lost knobs or hanging hinges on the doors.

25.

Jebez kills a man

I THOUGHT I WOULD NOT SURVIVE THIS ONE

JEBEZ'S LIFE WAS HEADED in a very positive direction; he had a good paying job, nice apartment, wife and a wonderful baby, plenty of food in the refrigerator, his own auto and a motor cycle. But the girls kept calling me telling me that he had a gun. I knew that was bad news because he has a temper. I kept telling him to get rid of that gun. Some months later on a Sunday after-noon in December; before Christmas; The phone rings and my oldest daughter say in distress; MOMA-! "Jebez shot a man! I could not breathe. When I caught my breath; I said; What? Not my Jebez.

After he was arrested all kind of stories came out. People who were not there said they had seen it all. The people who did see the shooting told conflicting stories. He said it was self defense. A fight broke out; a knife was pulled, the man spit on him. DNA did find the spit on his clothes, but he said his aim was to shoot in the air. He never meant to kill any one. Jebez went to trial and was sentence; fourteen to twenty years. I thought was not going to make it. He unlike Mickey; were entirely two different people. He never gave me any trouble. He had just returned home from the Army and got married. He lived his baby Girl. All the elderly people adored him; He was always helping people. He took after my father; he can do and fix just about anything. Our prayers got him an early release. He lost his wife, his child and his dignity. His life took a complete turn around; and has life has never been the same. He was tall, black, thin, and handsome. He has never been the same. He really did love his wife. She came to my house with her Brother and took all his stereo equipment that he brought from Okinawa, and got a divorce and remarried and had several more children. She was his wife; what could I say. I gave it to her. Jebez was furious. He asked; "why did you give up my equipment; I brought that from over Seas".

No matter what the reason; when one take another's life; that blood forever cries out. And Prison is not a rehabilitation center. However there are some who should never be released. But most of those who are released lose their dignity. Instead of being independent; they become dependent.

His wife gave their daughter away to a couple who kept her away from us. They even told her lies about us. When Jebez was released from prison he was on parole. He kept trying to see his daughter, her Guardians told him if he came back to try to see her again; they would call his parole officer and report him as a trouble maker. So he had to back off. When she got grown; and both Guardians had passed away. Now she knows the whole truth. It is never too late for good things to happen. Knowing the truth will set you free. She knows both sides of the story. One should never make a decision; until you know both sides of the story. There is always; your side, their side, and the truth.

Back with WT

WT did not like living alone. That was our excuse for getting back together. He moved in with me. This caused him to drive eighty miles to work each day. Forty miles further than when he lived in the Condo. He rented the Condo, for a while; but the tenant did not pay the rent as agreed, so he sold it. We were doing ok; then we started getting into arguments about love making. We were arguing about sex and he threw a cup of coffee into bed on me; and stormed out to work. When he comes home we both act as if nothing had happen; neither one of us ever held grudges. WT was a happy type of person and enjoyed life; he enjoyed taking me places, even though he drove to the City every day; we had no problems going back to the City for all our recreations. We did not visit any of the clubs where we lived. The women there did not get a chance to know very much about him. He had dated a couple of ladies there before we met. After he came back from the Nam; it was him and me. We were out of town every week end, but the intimacy needed much help

Jahari's Brother; the Pastor went into the hospital for a complete check-up. As he was getting dressed to come home; he got a blood clot and died instantly. We could not believe it. I could always go to him when I needed to borrow money; because he knew I was a woman of my word. Not only for that reason; but he was a great person to know and a great Brother-in-Law.

WT's PREMONITIONS

Big Sis had met a very young male friend. He had a friend he wanted me to meet name Guy because we were older woman, they thought we had money. Instead of going home from work one evening; I stopped at the bar. Something I never did. Guy came into the bar and we began to talk. We decided to go up on the hill to use Big Sis's house while she was at work. She worked afternoons. I called her and got permission. WT was not home from work yet. After Guy and I had been in her house for a while; we heard some one walking in side the house. They'd go from room to room. The person had passed our door while checking out the bath room. He passes our room again and went up stairs.

He came back down stairs Guy had gotten up and was putting on his clothes. WT looks in the room but it was dark. He had his gun in his hand. He had come up to her house looking for me. His instincts led him up there. I was totally shocked. I just knew we would be safe up there. We lived on the west side of town and she lived a ways from us on the Hill. After WT saw the man; he just walked out and got into his car and left. I was afraid to go home so I went down to my daughter's house. Guy called WT from her house and threatened him. Telling him he would put his boys on him. WT being in the Army; could not stand any trouble on his record. I was not in agreement with Guy making those threats because Guy was not my man. I went home before WT moved out. I tried to explain; but he was not hearing anything from me. He even took the refrigerator he had purchased.

WT moved out that next day; and got an apartment in the City. Guy moves in with me. After WT cools off; we start talking again; and

I was up at his place every week end. He would lay out the red carpet for me. He would cook me a nice dinner; and make mad love to me. He always knew how to win me back. WT would do all the things when we were separated; that he should be doing while we are together. Guy would be at my house waiting for me while I would be spending the week-end with WT. Guy got tired of waiting for me, and moved out. He moved in with some one else.

WT and I were seeing each other periodicity when he told me he had gotten some one pregnant. He said it was something that just happens. I know making a baby is not something that just happens. I was begging for his love and affections while we were together; and he had the Gould to go sleep with some one else. When he said to me; "it is time for me to give you my name; I did not want his name; nor did I ever want to see him again. So we broke up. But WT would still call me. When Jebez got in trouble; he said he had a feeling something was wrong; so he called that same evening. He came to my rescue; and took me out; to try and calm me down. I was devastated. After that he would come and spend almost every night. He was at my house when the baby was born, a boy. He got the call that she was in labor. He waited until time to go to work that next morning. Then he went to see the baby. When he came back that evening, he told me it was a boy

I got a call one Sunday morning that My Sis; the Pastor's wife was dead. She had hit a tree on her way to church. She had always said; she didn't want to live with out her husband. Rumor had it that she was forced of the street into the tree by a truck. However the crash killed another person too. So many things were happening. WT and I broke it off; we lost touch with each other. I was too hurt to keep seeing him. I didn't like him any more. I felt Invaded. I thought I could never forgive him. I found out; it's not time that changes things; it's your mind and heart. One of the great things I can say about WT is; he looked out for his son, mentally, physically, and financially until he was grown.

26.

My own Beauty Shop

OH HAPPY DAY

I DECIDED I NO longer wanted to work away from home. I always wanted to work out of my home, and be my own boss. I talk to Santa Claus about it; he did all of his business with a certain bank; and he knew the manager very well. He gave me the manager's name and told me to go tell him he sent me; and tell him my story, and he was sure he would give me the loan. I did just that; and I got the loan. Then Santa sent a man who was said to be a carpenter to build the Shop on to my house. The house was on a corner lot; there were plenty of room to add on a beautiful Beauty Shop.

Santa didn't know this was a person who played the horses.; he also didn't know; he would come to me for money for materials, and I did not know that I wasn't suppose to give it to him; so I would give what he ask for. He would use it to play the horses until the money was gone. He had used all the money I had borrowed for materials; to build the Shop. He had another man helping him to do the work with him. He did not tell me what was going on until there was no more money to finish the work. His helper stayed on out of guilt; because he said, he should have told me. He worked and did whatever he could so that I could open the shop. I had a dead line to open. Some times the helper would get some lumber from some discount place to fix the part the Carpenter didn't finish. Every week when I got paid; I would buy what I could in

136

the line of materials. The shop was never professionally finished. It was just a botched up room; but there was plenty of love in that Shop. The Customers found no fault in it. They got what they needed. At one time rumor had it that Cosmetologists would have to add Sociology in their professnal studies; because we hear a lots of problems.

After the loan was granted, and I had received the check from the bank; they had made a mistake and the check was more than I was approved for, therefore my payments were not calculated for the amount I received. My loan agreement said one amount and the check said another. I call the bank and informed them of the mistake. The manager asks if I would have any problem making the payments. I said of course not. The payments didn't change. I paid if off on time with no late payments. I thought this would put me on the road to build my credit. I needed more money from the bank to finish the room. I went back for another loan; but that Manager had retired. The Manager who had replaced him was so rude to me. He would not even talk to me. I could not imagine why they would not accommodate me since I had such good paying record. They had given me too much money; and I paid it off without any problems. That was their mistake.

That summer the Police shot and killed my Son-in-law's fifteen year old brother because he was running; and they thought he was the young man they were chasing. He was shot in the back. Some Pastors; from the NAACP gathered some of us church and lay members to march on the Court House. I joined in the march; and was blacked balled for marching. This Police officer was gun happy. In those days the NAACP was active. He had done so much stuff; that the organization was asking for the Chief's resignation. Some of the other marchers experienced similar treatment as I did. We found out that was why I could not obtain another loan. No banks or Finance Companies would loan me any money. The Shop still needed lots of work to get it in operation. The helper was still trying to do what he could to help me open my shop. The windows weren't finished; and I had no steps. I called a Minister; who was a carpenter; he said he would build some steps for me for a small fee. I said ok. The porch was five feet from the ground. He built a ladder instead of steps. My customers could not walk up that ladder. I would have been sued for sure. He charged me one hundred dollars for a ladder instead of steps. I did not pay him. I got in touch with another

Carpenter who specialized in concrete to build some concrete steps for me. The steps that lead into the house where I lived were new steps already in place; but I needed steps to enter into the Shop. I thought I had made that very clear as to where I wanted the new steps to begin.

When I got home, they had built a concrete porch; instead of steps, and coverer the new steps over with the concrete. They charged me four hundred dollars. The porch was connected across from door to door. So I made the best of a bad situation. I would go across the porch to the shop. The shop had its own door; that way I could lock the shop when I finish work. It also had its bad points too. When the snow fell and would freeze; that porch was very slippery. I almost slipped and fell twice in my high heel shoes on that ice. Everybody was taking my money for messed up work. I was still working at the Comb.

I kept trying to get a loan to finish the shop. I could not give up. That was where I would work and make my living. I finally got the Shop open enough to work in it. All of my customers followed me. Thank God; I did not have to build a clientele. They were all were standing appointments. I practiced what I had learned in Beauty School. I did not visit on the phone while at work. I was on time and looking professional. If a customer was more than fifteen minutes late; they had to reschedule. I booked my clients every hour. I later enrolled in my Friend's School to get my degree in hair weaving. I almost did not make it, because we were talking. It was a three day class and the class cost one hundred dollars a day. On that last day I ask God to help me, because I was not getting it. On that last day; it opened up to me. I asked the instructor if she knew anyone who had weaved their own hair. She said she knew of one person. That was all I needed to know. I went home and stood in front of the mirror and ask the Holy Spirit to show me how to weave my own hair. I was tired of spending mega dollars for other people putting that bad hair on my head like hay. The Holy Spirit showed me step by step, and I weaved my own hair for many years until it could not take the stress any more.

THE WINDOW

Guy was still trying to hang around. One night I was at home on the phone talking to Rusty, whom I had dated off and on. We would see each other every blue moon. He called and asked if he may come over. I said yes I'd like to see you. He came by and spent a few hours we even went into the bedroom. We talked about Marriage. We had known each other for years; since I was a kid. We grew up in the same area. We even had talked about getting married some years back; but he had started drinking. That was not something I could deal with. After he left; Guy open the door and came into the kitchen where I was. He had come through the crawl space window and sat on the top steps the whole time. The bed room was right across a three foot wide hall. That door and the bed room door were right cross from each other. He had heard every thing we talked about. I pretended not to be frightened; but I was frightened out of my skin. He had access to both of us. Rusty always carried a gun. We talked; and he told me what he heard; and he left. I didn't expect to see him again because we had already parted friendship and he really should not have been there. We were not to see each other again, so it was over for me. I know I got me some Angels watching over me; as Rev. André Crouch sang that song; and I can sing it too. Guy kept dropping by. He was always asking to borrow money; because he gambled. I loaned him money twice, and he did not pay me back. I wasn't giving up my hard earned money. I worked from nine o' clock A.M. to sometimes twelve p.m. Cosmetology work is not easy. One of the ladies Guy was seeing would make appointments with me to get her hair done to be close to him. I could have poured some lye in her eyes. I thought if she was that desperate; I needed to let her have him, so I did. Guy did not want to let it go. I really had fallen for him. I had not seen him for a few days; I got lonely for him. I went to the liquor store and purchased a half pint of old grand dad and drank the whole bottle. I was so sick; I prayed to God if he would let me get through that feeling; I will never let my emotions cause me to do that to my self again ever. I kept my promise to God. I got control of my thoughts.

Guy finally came by and we had an argument; he put a gun in my mouth because I said it was over between us. I could not go through what I had just experienced ever again. The lady he was seeing got pregnant; thinking that would trap him. No woman could trap Guy. He was tall and very handsome. I think he was insecure; because he didn't have material things. How could any one that handsome be so insecure? He was very cold. I never knew how to under-stand him. When I'd meet some one; it seems nobody was interested in him before me; but as soon as I show him how to dress; and we'd be seen together; then the women wanted him. Guy didn't have changing clothes. I left him as I found him. The women were after him like a dog after a bone. I was finally able to server that relationship for good. I figured; if he was so popular let those ladies supply his needs.

The shop began to leak. I did not have any money to pay the helper; so we had to work out a deal in which to pay him.. He really stuck with me to help open my shop. I guess he felt sorry for me; because he did not warn me that the Carpenter was taking my money to the tracks. I paid different people hundreds of dollars to fix that roof. Every month I was dipping into my pay check paying people to patch the roof. No body could stop the leak. Every body was just patching spots. It needed a whole roof. I could not get a loan from anyone. The helper finally realized he could not do any more to help; so he vanished.

27.
Meeting my third husband

SOME OF US GOT together and created a Bowling team. It consisted of five people; three men and two women. We were part of a bowling League. Our team bowled two nights a week. One of the fellows on my team name was Jacob. They voted me to be team Captain. The other lady was so funny. She made the team. We were a good team. Some weeks Jacob would be ill and in the hospital. I would always check on my people to see why they missed bowling. The League would go once a year to bowl against other Leagues. We had been a team two years before Jacob asks me for a date. I was surprised; because I was eleven years his senior. He was separated when we met. He said he had told his wife; if she left him again; that would be the end of the marriage. I guess she didn't believe him. So she left. He said; "all the other times when she would leave; and if she saw him talking to a female; she would walk up show her authority and scare her away". He said;☺" when he was eighteen; he saw me at a club; and said; "that Lady is going to be my wife". That club was the last to close on week-ends to close; it was call, the After Hour Club.

I always changed the conversation when he would bring up the subject. He broke his foot riding his Motor Cycle. He would come to the alley on his crutches and hang around while we bowl. He was determined to take me out. I finally consented. I was very surprised. Jacob was a real gentleman. He took me to a very exclusive club. The evening was eccentric. That was the beginning of a lasting relationship.

We didn't want to live apart; gradually he moved in. He was a Mild natured person, and very even tempered, and never raised his voice. He became my shining Armor.

Guy tried to nullify the relationship between Jacob and me. He would come by my house periodicity while Jacob would be there; saying he needed to talk to me. He would also show up at the bowling alley. One time he asks Jacob if he may have a word with him. They talked; but Jacob never told me what they talked about. Guy told me; "he told Jacob; he'd better treat me right. I told him he had his nerves: because he did not know how to treat me. About a month later the phone rings about two a: m. I answer half sleep; Guy is screaming for me to come get him; that some one is shooting at him. He says, "he is in a near by phone booth; and I needed to come get him". I called 911 and reported what he had said to me. The Police checked it out and called back and said, "It was a Hokes". The next day Jacob said to me; "if I had gone to check out that call; that would have been the end of our relationship". He said, "It is up to the woman to end the relationship". I agreed. I severed that relationship for good. I never saw Guy again.

One year three of us Ladies were chosen to go to Las Vegas to bowl in a Tournament. We did not win, but it was fun. That was my first time there. We went site seeing to the Hoover Dam. That was really exciting and also scary. That Dam is awesome. They had Escorts to guide the Tourists through it. We played the slots, and the food is delicious in Vegas. We really enjoyed it. Jacob and I had to stop Bowling when he got ill.

THE RACCOON IN THE SHOP

I was still trying to obtain a loan to have the roof repaired on the Beauty Shop. It had leaked for years. The wood had rotted and a hole was in the roof. One morning about 2 a: m; Jacob and I were wakening by a noise in the Shop. We thought it was a burglar. He got the Flash light; we went into the Shop; turned the lights on; there was a big Raccoon with his eyes shining like glass. Jacob caught him by the tail and took him to the over pass and let him go. There was a tall tree beside the house; the Raccoon had climbed the tree, got onto the roof; and fell into the Shop through that hole. Jacob and I lived together until his divorce was finalized.

We were leaving the house one after noon; as we were making a u-turn from our house heading out; surprisingly who drives up? It was WT. I got angry when I saw him. I told him we were leaving the house; what do you want? He said, "I just came by". He did not know about Jacob until then. In the pass; everybody had to go when WT showed up. I knew that day it was over between us. Jacob's Cousin; asked him if he loved me. He said, "Yes I do" the cousin said; "marry her; don't keep living together". We set our date. Jacob's Ex had been calling all hours of the night harassing me, calling me all kinds of terrible names. I was ok with that, because those were not the names my mother named me.

We left the bowling alley and stop by the chicken place to get something to eat. Every body had to stand out side to place their orders. It had snowed enough to be a little slippery. While Jacob was standing out side waiting to receive his orders, I was waiting in the car. An automobile came into the parking lot at a high rate of speed. I looked over, and thought what fool would be driving so fast on that snow. It was his Ex. She had spotted the car. I locked the doors; then I remembered she had been calling me un-friendly names; so I un-locks the doors. I didn't want her to think I was afraid of her. If I had; the harassments would have never ended. She jumped out of her car, and opens my passenger door; where I was seated; she put her foot inside the car; and started asking me questions. I was answering her very calm and nice. Then she put her finger on my nose. It was already dark at night; but it got darker; because I was so angry; I could not contain myself. I got out of the car; and caught her in her collar. I really lost it for a moment. I had some rings on my fingers. I was punching her like a boxer. When I came to myself; Jacob was pulling us apart. He ordered her back into her car, and then he ordered me back into his car. She had been use to bulling every lady he talks to. We had no more problems with her. She would let his two kids come over, and tell them not to obey me. The older girl was cool; but the little one was rebellious. One day she decided to climb the tree in the yard. I told her to climb down. She said; "you're not my Mama, you don't tell me what to do". I got a little switch out of that tree and tanned those legs, because I was responsible for her safety while in my care. I also didn't want her to get hurt. I could not love Jacob and not love his kids. I never had any more mouth from her.

Some how; my kids heard about the fight. I don't know who told Mickey. I was so embarrassed. They said; "but mama she asked for that fight". Mickey laughed hysterically. That was a joke to him because that was how he survived. He did not bother anybody; but nobody could whip him fair. Jacob and I got married at our house. Our Pastor performed the ceremony. Louise was my Matron of Honor; his cousin was Jacob's best man. Both of our families, and my sun-in-law's family were all there. When Jacob's oldest daughter got grown, we got along fine.

Jacob had a cousin I had not met yet. He came to visit us one evening as we were getting ready to go bowling. He was a City slick kind of a guy. He went to the alley with us, but he didn't stay; he left right away, but he kept calling to see where we were. Jacob could not bowl in peace because he kept calling. When we got home our house had been broken into. Stereo receiver, turn-table and sewing machine were gone. We believed that Cousin did it. We only had one lock on our door. We think he noticed the lock while leaving our house. Our Insurance cancelled us; because of that one incident. I never found another sewing machine as strong and study as that one was. It was one of those old fashion singer sewing machines in the cabinet. They tool the machine from the cabinet.

THE GIRLS BEGIN TO MOVE OUT

The last two girls moved out into their own apartments. They all had had after school jobs. When they graduated they were blessed to be hired permanent. I had instilled in them; that when they turn eighteen; they must move out on their own, while I'm still alive; so that I can show them how to be independent... I talk to them constantly about immorality. I was not having my house filled with babies. It had been too hard raising them. I was not intending to raise any more kids. I taught them to pay me- to do their hair. Children need to be taught to be independent while still at home. Most African American kids are not taught anything about how to budget money. **I wasn't.** I learned the hard way after they came along and I had suffered awhile. They were grown; and it was five of them. I could not afford to do their hair free; however if they were short of funds; I would give them a break. But they did not make that a habit. I taught them; nothing is free; except Salvation; never the less we have to work it out.

Three of the girls got married after moving out. Two went to Collage. One daughter later decided to go and get her degree after marriage. There were divorces in our family. I was not any help in giving my children any advice about divorce; I had divorced their father. I had always been taught; that when you marry; if it doesn't work; get out and get a divorce. That is wrong advice. My life ended up in four divorces and six marriages before learning the real truth; so what could I tell them about divorcing. After Louise's divorce; while still in Collage she met the husband by whom they truly acknowledged their vows to the end; till death do we part. It was truly death that parted them. He was the son to me like my own. It was through him at our house gathering and discussing that we all came back to the Lord. We connected to his family and we all became one big family. Every holiday we all came together. His mother and his Aunts were some of the best cooks in the world. Those two could cook anything. They cause me to learn to eat foods I thought I did not like. One was pumpkin pie. I hated pumpkin pie until I ate theirs. After his Mother found out that I liked butter milk pie; she would make one especially for me every holiday. We never expected to loose him at such young age. When he went into the hospital; we just knew he was coming home. We are still connected with the family even though he is gone. His Mom and Aunts have joined him and we miss them.

My whole family has gone through divorces. After that first divorce it seems as though it became an obsession with me. I was going to get a divorce because Jacob hit my dog. I had a poodle when we met. I was always kissing the dog. He would say to me; don't kiss me; you been kissing the dog. She got in his way and he hit her. He was not trying to hurt her; he accidentally hit her in the eye. I got angry; I said; you don't hit my dog! I said; I'm getting a divorce went to our family lawyer to file for a it. The Lawyer talked me out of it. He told me about an incident that happened to his dog; because his son left him out all day in the hot heat without water. He said, "He was mad as hell". I was ok; I took his advice and went back home. I apologized to Jacob. He really was jealous of the dog. I had to go into great lengths to explain to him that my love for the dog was not the same as my love for him. He said, "Now I understand the difference". I can see how Exodus 20:5 was operation in our lives when God said; "I will punish the children for the sins of their Fathers, to the third and fourth generations". We've had divorces in our families as far back as I can remember. When I hear people say they have been married forty, fifty or more years; I bless that marriage; because that couple has fought the good fight of faith. If my first marriage had lasted with my kids father; we would have celebrated sixty two years of marriage in 2010; and he probably would still be here. (Although I don't know if I would.)SMILE

28.
The Call on my life

WHEN GOD BEGAN TO call me back to Him; I was in a Social Club with seven Ladies and I made eight. The name of the club was <u>The Elite Eight</u>. It was a Non-Profit social club. We would give dances at the various night clubs. At the end of the year, we would find a needed organization to donate the proceeds to. We did that about five years. All of our husbands would help. Near the end of the fifth year; my husband began to get ill. He was not able to do it any more. He had emphysema. Jacob didn't feel up to going out any more. I was still trying to hang out with the club members.

Every week-end we Ladies would get high and go out, but when the high wore off, I would be so board; I would call my husband to come pick me up. He would ask, "What's wrong? Aren't you having a good time? I would feel so guilty, I always enjoyed being out with my husband. He was at home ill; and I was out in the streets. I knew what it feels like to be at home and your spouse is out every week end. I had lived that life before. The guys would judge us ladies as to who they could ask for a dance. Seven of us would be dress up in our sophisticated attire; but one of us dressed in her jeans and looked comfortable, so to speak. Every time one came to our table for a dance they would ask her. I said; you don't see anybody else at this table? He said; "you dance? I said sure. He said; "I never would have thought you danced". I ask why? He said; "you'll looking so up tight and sophisticated; like you'll just came to look pretty". From then on we had no problem.

147

One Saturday night we Ladies were at our favorite Lounge. We were sitting at the table; and everybody had been asked to dance; then I was asked to dance. When I entered the dance floor, I could not find a step. My feet would not move. I had no rhythm. Right at that moment; I knew the answer. It was time for me to leave the night club for ever. It was God telling me it's time to come back to Him. All those years I had been asking God not to let me stay away from him too long. He was saying; "it is time; NOW!

I got back in church where my old Pastor was still pasturing. I rededicated my life back to God. I started to Sunday school every Sunday. I was flicking the T V one evening and came across this Great T.V. Minister. My life was never the same. My Pastor assigned me to be the woman's day Chair Lady. He assigns a great Lady to be Co-Chair to work with me. We worked so well together. We were told that that was the best woman's day program ever. We prayed about everything we set out to do. We became connected after that.

THE SET UP

My Mother-in-law, her two daughters and I were at the Smorgasbord having lunch. We were sitting in the booth next to two white ladies. We were talking about how men act sometimes. They joined in the conversation and we went into great lengths about life. We befriended each other. We exchanged phone numbers. The next day one of them called me and said she needed some one to talk to. We had communicated a few times after our first meeting. She called me one morning and asks me to come over; that she was depressed. I was always praying for people; so I got her address and went over. She lived on the East side of town. She was one of the ones who had not had a chance to get from that side of town yet. You know when you hear the East side; you know who mostly live on that side of any town.

She had me to touch so many things in her house. She showed me her bed room. She had me to open her refrigerator; just handing me things to touch. I did not think anything about it until I read the paper a few days later; she had shot her husband. I guess she was trying to get my finger prints on things to frame me. I'm sure she meant to kill him; and she would have my finger prints on everything. I don't know what happen after that. She never called again. When I got to thinking about that set up; I thought: suppose he had died. It would have been her word against mine. The devil was trying to set me up. He was mad because he had lost a soul.

God said Go get Uncle Jacob

Jacob had two uncles; He was name after the one; the other one was Uncle G. Uncle G had gotten Ill. While Uncle Jacob was taking care of Uncle G, he got ill and was hospitalized. My husband, his sister and I would go visit him. His Niece which was Jacob's sister was trying to tell him about Jesus; and he would Curse her out right there in the Hospital. I had met Uncle J when he worked as a bar tender at several of the night clubs. He had done that type of work for years. Everybody knew Uncle J. I did not know Uncle G. The Lady Uncle J married used to share living quarters years back at Big Sis's house when we all lived there. I was surprise to know that was his wife. We went way back.

After uncle J went home from the hospital Uncle G died, and he was not able to attend Uncle G's funeral. After the funeral; there was a re-pass in the lower level of the church. After the re-pass was over; Jacob and I were coming up to go to our car. The Lord spoke to me; and said go and lead Uncle J to Christ. I said; "OH NO! Not me Lord!" I told Jacob what I had just heard; he said; "go" I really prayed about that; because he was cursing his Niece right in the Hospital; as she was telling him about the Lord. I finally got my release to go. I called his wife and told her, what I was about to come over to do. She was so happy. She was a Christian already. She said; "he was so mean to her because of his pain. I walked into his bedroom; and spoke to him. I told him my testimony about how God had called me back out of a world of sin; and that Jesus told me to come and lead him to Christ. He said; "OK: I was shocked. I led Uncle J in the sinner's prayer; he cried, and he thanked me, I leaned over; we hugged and I left. His wife said he was a changed man and so peaceful until death a few weeks later. God always has his timing. All we have to do is to listen, and follow his timing and be obedient.

29.
My husband was dying too

HE REFUSED TO STOP SMOKING

MY HUSBAND WOULD GO to church with me when he felt better; soon his illness got the best of him. He was in and out of the hospital monthly. For months he could not lay down. He would lean on a portable bar we had in the living room. Even the oxygen did not help. The emphysema had collapsed his lungs. He still would not stop smoking. The doctor showed us what a lung looks like when it is diseased with emphysema because it is a form of cancer. It had the appearance of a burned black char broiled peace of meat. One of the times when Jacob was in the hospital he was so mean. I did not realize that pain will do that; so I told him I was not coming back to see him. The Doctor told me; "what ever you do, do not miss a day of visiting him". That let me know the seriousness of his illness. Of course I didn't mean it anyway. The Doctor knew how close his time was. I thought he was coming home, and would be with me much longer. He was so young. I know age has nothing to do with death. I just didn't want to let go. We had so much fun. He loved dancing and was full of laughter. I liked doing things to make him laugh. He would say to me; "I'm going to admit you to the nut house, because you're crazy"

Every time Jacob would go to the hospital, it would be me insisting he should go. This time he was leaning on the bar with his P.J's still on; he asks me to take him to the hospital. I knew it was over, because he never failed to get dressed, he always was neat as could be. When he asked to be taken to the hospital I knew he had taken all the pain he could stand. After we got him in and out of the emergency room into intensive care; we lost him for a few minutes, the nurses were calling for Code Blue. They were able to resuscitate him and put him on the machine for five days. After which he started to breathe on his own. He was put in a regular room for a few days. I thought he was getting better and would come home again.

Jacob knew he was never coming back home. He knew a missionary who was a friend of ours and she was also one of my Customers was in the room next to our room. Her husband was also ill. Jacob asks me to ask her to come and prey with him. She led him in the sinner's prayer once again. He said; "he wanted to be sure of where he was going". Then he got real bad and they put him back in intensive care. I would work in the Salon late some nights and go to the Hospital and spend the night with him in intensive care. I would sleep in the chair. No one ever called to see if I needed any help or relief. After a month of that I was worn, but God gave me strength to make it through. I tell people the decisions you make, not only affect you; but those around you and who loves you. As bad as my husband wanted to stay; he could not stop smoking. Cigarettes killed his baby sister a few years after him.

THE CALL TO THE HOSPITAL

One time he rose up and asks me to get in bed with him. I wanted to; but I thought that would be against the Hospital rules. A few mornings after that the nurse called me at home and said come to the Hospital. The same friend who own the Beauty School and I had been communication with each other. She had lost her husband two years before. She had called me and asks; "what you doing? I said the Hospital called; I am getting ready to go there. She said; "call me when you are ready". I never called her; she called back. I said I can't get together. She said wait; "I will be there". When we got there the Nurse said: call the family". I called his ex, so she could bring his two daughters. I called the rest of his family .It took his Children so long to get there. He was gone when they arrived. His Mom had died from emphysema a few years back. I had met his Mom before I met Jacob. She was one of the maids working at the Boston Store when I worked in the Salon. Some times we would have lunch together. She was a smoker. We never thought I would be her daughter-in-law and that she would not live to see it. His father deceased after I met Jacob.

30.

My new Automobile

God moved in spite of the bad credit

THE AUTOMOBILE WE HAD was falling apart. Jacob had asked his cousin to let me use one if his cars until I could get ours fixed. Jacob joined a life insurance on himself; but when he got ill; it took so long for him to get disability; I had to let it go. He was nearly dead before they would give him disability. I had struggled to keep up the insurance; because he was using marijuana for the pain; and that was costing big bucks. After Jacob passed; my Ray suggested, "That if it was the kind of policy that had been paid into long enough; that it was a possibility it might still pay; even though I had canceled it". We called the agent, he investigated; and it did pay. Ray and Jacob's Sister made all the plans for the Funeral.

I wanted to know more about Jesus. That T.V. evangelist along with a lot of radio ministers had lit my fire. Another Local Pastor had come out of the same church I was attending. He had started his ministry in the Holiday Inn. I started visiting along with my daughter and her husband. I like the way he teaches that word. I can get more from teaching than preaching.

I joined the Center. That Pastor dissects that word and makes it so plain; they could not pay you not to understand it. I heard at least three Pastors say, "Write down the vision". I also read it in Habakkuk 2: 2. So I learned to believe; what ever you need write it down; pray on it and confess it night and day; it will come to pass; if it be God's will; and you have faith to believe it. I had much faith because I was sitting under great teaching. My Pastor would tell me that I had a greater opportunity to lead many more people to Christ than he; because of the type of business I was in. I really did lead many people into the sinner's prayer. The Beauty Shop was an all you need place. I tried to cater to people needs; it was not all about the money.

CONFESSIONS BRINGS POSSESSIONS

I needed a car. I wrote down the color, make, model, and all the accessories, I wanted; Metallic silver, with a moon roof. I needed to make it as complicated as possible; so I would know this auto when I saw it. Back then they did not make the autos with the moon roofs from the factory. The reason I needed to know this car when I see it, was because my credit was so **bad** it would have to be God. That is why you must write down your vision. I was still driving our cousin's car. On our way to the City; the teacher friend and I dropped her bad lemon car off at the Dealership and went on our way. On the way back; we were wondering, what would be the lesser red tape, to lease or to purchase an Automobile. We decided to stop in at the Dealership to get some information. The Salesman met us at the door to assist us. He told us; "leasing was much more complicated".

He asked what kind of auto was I interested in. I told him I was looking for a 1984 Riviera; he said, "we don't have any left; we don't have any for our side walk sale coming up'. He suggested we take a walked out back with him to be sure. There was one Riviera left, but that was not what I had written down, and it had a sold sign on it, and it was not the color. So as we were leaving the building, a Sales person turned into the lot driving so- fast, I thought he was going to run into the building. He jumps out of the car runs right up to me, and said; "do you want it". "We ordered it for a demo, but if you want it we won't put any more miles on it; it's yours".

MY NEPHEW THOUGHT I HAD LOST IT

My nephew was also one of the Salesmen working there, but he was out to lunch when we got there. He was returning just in time to ask if I wanted to take the car for a test drive. For some reason I said, I may as well. As I drove the car onto the interstate; I realize; this is the car I had written down and confessed. It had everything I had written down except the moon roof. I started screaming, THIS IS IT! THIS IS IT! My Nephew was seated in the back seat, and the Teacher was in front with me. He thought I had lost it. He did not know the full story at that time.

The two youngest Daughters worked at General Motors. I called Knee Baby and told her about the car, and the price they were asking, she told me what the going price was; and don't pay any more than that for it. My Nephew and I started in with the negotiations. They went on for a while the Boss did not want to accept my offer. Finally He said; "Aunt Mag, what is it going to take to sell you this car? I said; only the price I'm offering. They finally agreed to accept my offer. They even allowed me to trade in that broke down Lincoln, and add the moon roof at no additional cost. You would think I had money and good credit the way I was negotiating. That is the way one should act when you know who you are in Christ.

Because my credit was bad, I was being financed through one of those; when you have bad credit companies. My payments were going to be four hundred and seventy five dollars monthly. When I went to transfer my insurance to the new auto, my insurance agent asked if I knew that they finance autos. She said don't worry; "we will take it from here". So they financed the auto for only three hundred and twenty five dollars a month.

This was a 1985 Riviera silver that I confessed and prayed about for ten months. I purchased an 85 Riviera in 19 84. I anointed the car and blessed it. I'm glad I did; because I took my Grand- daughter to work one after noon at a Nursing Home. I pulled up behind an elder gentleman as he was ready to back up. He did not see me; and backed into my passenger door where she was seated. I screamed (JESUS). He pulled up and we all three jumped out to look at the damage, there weren't any. We all started to shout thanking God. One Sunday some one stole my car from the church while we were in service. Because of the anointing; the thieves could not get away; they ran into a fence right around the corner from the church and left it there. That was easy for the police. I only had to repair one front fender.

MEETING NEW FRIENDS

The new Church Center I had joined. I met two Ladies and every Sunday after service we would go out to dinner. One Sunday after we had returned from dinner, we were still parked in front of the church. One Lady began to tell us that she would miss our outings when she gets married. I asked; are you getting married. She said; "I'm, um; yea". She was a little hesitant. I said let's pray about it and see what God say. As we began to pray, I saw in a vision her and the groom standing under a big Beautiful tree. The grass was green, no houses, just beautiful green grass as far as one could see. Her dress was a long lace egg shell in color. She was getting married under this big tree. I could not tell who the Groom was. After the prayer ended, I told her what I had seen. She was so excited. "She said that was a confirmation, because that was the kind of dress she already had on lay-a-way". I did not know about any of her plans. We had just met each other.

They were united through her sister's dreams; which her sister had had many times about them. They all had gone to school together while growing up. She had no idea who her husband would be; but by faith she knew God had heard her prayer. The husband to be had lost his wife in death some time ago before the two of them came in contact. When the two of them met they both knew that; their meeting was a Divine order. After a month, they began to talk about setting a date. When Sister Girl told her future husband that everything was already set to go, he was amazed. He was expecting to set a date in order to get things ready. She had all her flower girls; they had their dresses, and everything it took to have a beautiful wedding all ready. She didn't know who; but she knew God had sent her angels to get him. That is faith.

She asked me to be her wedding coordinator, but my husband had only passed away eight months before, and I was getting ready to move to another State. By the time of her wedding I had moved. She sent me pictures of the wedding. It was beautiful. She gave me one of her eight by ten wedding photos; which I still have. They are still together.

THE WRONG MOVE

The Beauty Teacher and I drove to Alabama to visit Maggie. She was employed by the Government; and was transferred from California there by her job.

While we were there; we decided to check out employment in the Beauty Business. We found a Caucasian Beauty Business that needed a teacher and an operator. Sense she was a Cosmetology teacher, and I was an Operator; we jumped on the deal. It was a jump too soon. I was not supposed to deviate from my original plans. I was to visit my daughter, and after going back home; put my furniture in storage, come back and live with her to check and see if I might be able to build a clientele in my Profession. The owner of the Salons was building some apartments, and he said; "he would rent to us for a very low monthly rate". We decided between the two of us; that was a great deal.

This was in the month of April. The apartments were to be ready for us to move into by July. The end of June; I called the Manger to confirm everything. He said, "All is well". I rented my house to be occupied by August. In July I rented a twenty six foot truck. My oldest Grand Daughter helps me pack my furniture; and the teacher was packing her stuff. She didn't take lots with her. One of My Son-in Law's drove the truck from Ill to Alabama. It was scotching hot that day. I had to make sure I kept the car cool because I had my little poodle dog. The Teacher suffered with Bronchitis and by the time we arrived; she had gotten too sick to help us un-load the truck.

We had to wait in the hot sun until the Land-Lord got there to let us into the apartment. The apartments were a ways out in the Country from where he had to travel. After we were settled in; the next day I had to take The Teacher to find a Doctor to get a prescription. My sun-in-law decided to check on some jobs while he was there. Nothing was available. He took a flight back home. After getting settled in; we started our job with our Land lord. I would drop the Teacher off at the School; and I would go on to the Salon. We would stay all day.

At the Salon; the receptionist would make sure to take turn to send each operator a client. There were four operators; I was the only Afro American. Every body was trying to build a clientele. My booth was number four. One of the girls was German, she was tall stocky; and very pretty. She did all she could to help me stay. She and I went to lunch together each day. We all like working together; but it wasn't working out so well. There just were not enough clients coming into the Salon. We found out there had been some problems before we got there. All the Operators were new. While I worked there I had the opportunity to lead a young man to Christ. He gave me his favorite broach that he used in his hair shows. He traveled all over to different Cities to do shows. He had a case full of broaches; but that was his favorite one. At first he had said; "pick any other one you want". Except the one I had picked. He said; "not that one" He later changed his mind, and gave me the one I wanted. He thanked me for showing him what the word of God said about his life style.

The Teacher wasn't doing so well at the School either. We tried ethnic Shops. I was told later; it is never good to make a big decision after loosing a spouse in death, or if you are self-employed. It takes too long to build a clientele; especially moving from the Midwest to the Southern parts of the United States. If you are depending on women to help you build your clientele; and they don't know you; and they think you are attractive; and looking younger than your years; you can most definitely forget it. I could not build my business there. Women are very slow about helping one another. I hate meeting a sister and she has judged me at a distance. When you are close enough to speak; she will turn her head to avoid speaking. We advertised on one of the most listened to black radio stations; and nothing happened.

I was also an Herbal Distributor. I had become Supervisor with the Company before moving there. I really made a terrible mistake because people of all nationalities were purchasing the product from me. They were coming from miles away. I thought people every where wanted to be healthy and beautiful; and moving wouldn't make a difference to my Business; but I was wrong. I lost that business; because I would let some people have the products on credit and never got paid for it.

31.

Purchasing my house

THE TEACHER AND I met a realtor who befriended us. We would meet with her for lunch often, and just hang out. She had a great deal on a beautiful three bed room Tri-Level red brick; with an in ground swimming pool, two car garage and a fenced in yard. It was in a mixed quite neighborhood with Pecan trees in the yard. I had enough Money to put down on the house, and sustain me a few months. I was still hoping to find work

I asked the Teacher if she would get her own apartment. Her kids could not under stand why we needed to split our living arrangement. It's very hard for women to live together for whatever reason. We were getting a little aggravated with each other. I had begun to feel as if I was the total decision maker. I did not want to loose her friendship. I knew that is what would have happen if we had continued to live together. Thank God our friendship is still strong because I made that choice.

When our lease was up; I notified the Land Lord. He came to inspect the apartment; he got angry with me because I had accidentally spilled some make-up about the size of a fifty cent piece; on the carpet right by my dresser. I used everything that was recommended to me. Even stuff that was known to remove spots; nothing worked. He said my little poodle had caused the spot. We moved out with him being angry about the spot. I was very sorry about that; because when we moved in every thing was new. We were the first tenants to move in.

159

The complex was built on red mud. When it rain; it was so hard not to track that red mud in; but we manage not to. That was the only spot.

My plan was to move my shop to my house.. I could not find any one whom I could afford to pay to do the pluming. People would promise to come do it and charge less than professional prices. But they never showed up. Many times I would stay home waiting for people who promised they would come and hook up the shampoo bowl; but never show up. I did all I could to keep that house. It was beautiful and maintenance free. The payments were very low. I even thought about getting a male partner to move in with me; but I knew that would not be the right thing to do. If I wanted God's blessings I must stay within His will.

Moving Back Home

My Neighbor who lived a few houses down the street hated to see me leave. His wife had been ill for some months. I was invited to come pray for her after he saw I was a Christian. He loved to come down and talk to me about how he should get his life together with God. He enjoyed hearing the word from me. I invited him to go to church with me. My church had services twice a week. He never did go. I was beginning to meet other neighbors. The first week I moved into the house; I had received a call from WJ. I had set up my phone to transfer all my calls to my new number. He said; "he had called my house and got that recording". He said; "he and his buddy were going to be coming to Alabama that week end and that he wanted to stop and see me". I was so sure that I was strong enough in the Lord to lead him to Christ. He dropped his buddy off at his relatives, and came on to my house. I was happy to see him. I had not seen him in a few months. We went grocery shopping. WJ could not stop complementing on what a beautiful house I had. His job was in electrician; before he retired, so he connected all of my components and equipment. I had purchased a big Sate-Lite dish, and had it installed in my back yard. I loved watching the dish move around. My recreation room was level with my back yard.

After dinner; I brought the conversation to him about salvation. WJ said; "no one ever taught him about Jesus. I was determined to get him saved. Other words I found out; it is easier to pull one off the table; than to pull one up on the table. I was trying to pull him up on the table; instead I got pulled off the table before he left. He visited two days. That was a great mistake. WJ was still single and said he was still unsure about getting married again. He was still hung up on the material things he lost through his other two marriages. He dwelt on what he lost; and is still single. I was happy that we didn't hook up. He likes to argue and bring up old stuff. It wasn't hard to figure out why he was divorced.

MEETING DAVID

I met a young man name David at a Thrift store. I was so bored hanging around the Beauty Shop doing nothing. I decided to get away alone; which was something I was never able to do sense moving there. He came into the store; and walked over where I was. He said; "he was looking for some trousers, and he was in the Army". I asked why he needed clothes from a Thrift store. I think he saw me go into the store. We talked a while, he asked where I worked. I told him about the Shop I was spending my days in; but not my address. He came to the Shop one day and took me to lunch. Teacher and I would change Shops in mid-stream. When we saw nothing was happening at that Shop; we would move and try another one. We no longer were working at the place where David came the firs time. We moved to another Shop with the promise of building a good Business. After being there a month or two; nothing was happening there either. We tried four different Salons. I was board and needed to get out. The Door opens and there stands David. He had found out what Salon we had moved to. I was happy to see anybody to rescue me. He took me out to lunch. I started allowing him to come by the house. He knew how to give good messages; he would rub me down in oil. He found my G spots. I did not know where they were; or that I had any. Eventually I allowed him to pull me off that table. Then there was a little Minister; who got out of his place. What I learned from all of that is we can say what we have not done; never say what you want do. I also learned don't stray away from the flock. The Lion seeks the prey that is out side of the herd; walking alone. He has a better chance to attack. I was finding my way to the flock, but there were no fellowshipping. Most places of worship are so clickish. If they don't know you; you are all a lone. It took some repenting, time praying, and confessing Gods word.

The Thoughts in my head said it's been four years. You need this relationship, and you know you want to keep this house. I knew who was putting those thoughts in my head; but the flesh got weak. That's the way the spirit of darkness operates. After you slip; then he will put so much guilt in your conscious; in order to get you to say; what is the use of trying; because I have messed up, and God don't love me anymore. But I realized; If God did not bless me with that house; I didn't need it. I did not consult him about buying it. I just needed peace, and needed to get out by myself. The deal on the house was too good to pass up.

WE LOOSE LOVE ONES BECAUSE OF CONDEMNATIONS

We lost Maggie because she never felt worthy; to believe and ask God to heal her, If we can't forgive ourselves; we can't see God forgiving us. She ran to the church looking for help; and she was rejected there too. I know what it feels like to mess up when you have tasted the goodness of God. I was crying while I was messing up. God heard me and forgave me and brought me back to the fold. He showed me He can be my Spiritual husband until he gave me my earthly husband. I have never known what it feels like to be hugged and kisses and told; "I love you" but He teaches me how to give love, because He lives in me. The Realtor gave all the money back to me I had put down on the house. The only money I lost was the closing cost. That was favor. I had never heard of anything like that

I rented a truck and my Son-in Law; the knee baby's husband came down and drove the truck back to Illinois. I still had my house; it was rented out, but they agreed to move. I was able to notify them in time for them to find a place.

BELIEVING GOD FOR MY MATE

After I got settle and was back a while; I began to feel a little lonely. I always thought that I would not want to marry again There would never be anyone else like Jacob. It was now five years since he died. Sister Girl and I became prayer partners. She said if the Lord did it for her he would do it for me. Every day we would talk, pray, and confess my husband.

I wrote down what type of husband I wanted. In my couscous mind, as I was writing I think I really wanted someone like WT, but

I didn't like him. I can't explain how he compared to the person I was writing about; but I didn't think about WT being my husband. We had not heard from each other in fourteen years. Sister Girl kept on me to go get my dress and have every thing ready the way she did. I understood when you ask God for something according to his will you have to act like you have it; but my faith was more in healing not a husband. She finally won after two years. We set out to the Bridal Shop. We went to the one where she purchased her dress, but they were closed for vacation. So we went up the street to another one. As soon as we open the door there on a manikin was the dress I had in mind. It was the color, the length, and size. I tried it on, it was perfect. The Sales Lady said; "no one had noticed the dress since she hung it there". I wore head bands a lot. Sister Girl thought that is what I needed to wear on my head for my wedding. She asked the Lady to show her some bands while I was trying on the dress. She said; "I have this one that has been discontinued and is on sale. That was the one. It matched the dress perfect.

I put them in the lay-a-way. The Lady asked; "when is the wedding? We replied; we don't know. We don't even know who. Then we shared Sister Girl's testimony with her, and she was astounded. I made payments on the lay-a-way. I was not in a hurry to get it out. Almost two more years passed. Nothing was happening. I had gained a little weight;

Breaking my arm.

I decided to do something to pass the time. A lady I associated with was a skater. I went to the rank with her a few times. I love to watch them skate. She was an excellent skater. It was always something I wanted to do. In the south the only skating we could do; was on ice if we ever got any. So I decided to purchase a pair skates and she suggested I should take some lessons. She got me in touch with an instructor. After a few lessons; my instructor warned me not to go out on my own alone; but there was a skating rank thirty five miles away that had a special area for beginners. I tried to find some one to go with me. To no avail, I went for two weekends alone and every thing went well. I met a nice man the first night. He helped me and would hold me up to get me start rolling. Two week ends; he meet me there. On the third visit it was very crowded. People flowed over into the beginner's area. It got really crowded. I don't know where my helper had gone; he was not around. I never knew his name. I had been ministering to him. He said he was a Jew. I had prayed to get a chance to minister to some Jews. God said; "pray for the peace of Jerusalem". He would talk to me about how much he loved his wife; but she was an alcoholic. I was sharing Christ with him so he could get saved and minister to her. I was making some progress at least; He was listening. All of a sudden; somebody accidentally tripped me; when I came to myself; I was on the floor with a broken wrist. The fellow that I had been sharing with soon saw what had happened and came to help me off the floor. I did not know anybody there. I don't know what I would have done if he had not helped me. Nobody else noticed, or saw what had happen. That skating rank was too crowded that Friday night.

That gentleman went to my locker got my shoes. He helped me get them on; and helped me to me car. He tried to get me to go to the near by hospital, but I decided to drive the thirty five mile to the hospital in my home town. I reach the hospital's ER around 2:a.m. The nurse who waited on me; went to get some other nurses to come see the lady who had driven thirty five miles all alone in excruciating pain.. I ask what all the excitement was about; they said; "you could have passed out behind the wheel". I had never heard that before. The Orthopedic surgeon was not due in until three that after noon. I went home to wait for the Surgeon to come in. I went back at three that afternoon. He put a cast from my fingers to my under arm.

MY FAITH WAS WANING

Thank God it was my left wrist, because I had no one to help me. I learned to cook my food; but I could not take care of my Customers. My Pastor announced in Church that I needed some one to do my customers and help me out financially. Sandy and I was the only Cosmetologist in the congregation. Sandy volunteered to do my Customers; and gave me all the monies paid to her from each customer. That is how I survived those eight weeks. Sandy was Caucasian but she could do all types of hair. I realized what a friend really was. I had not ever experienced that type of friendship before. All my Customers were willing to go to her to help me out.

SISTER GIRL'S WORD FROM THE LORD

I got back to work and still did not really believe that a husband was in the making for me. Sister Girl had asked the Lord one day as she prayed, would He please give her something to tell me; that would build my faith. I had stop believing; because where I lived; the men in that area were not marring material. All the good men were already taken. I wanted some one who loved the Lord. Mostly ladies filled the churches then and still do. One evening she called me at work; and said "Sister Maggie" Very excitedly" (that's what she calls me). "Who do you know; whose name is; and she called at least three of the first names that started with W's. She said the Holy Spirit was giving them to her so fast; she couldn't catch anything but parts of the first names. I said to her. I only know two persons with those first names; one of them do not own up to knowing anything about the Lord. He said he was not taught anything about Jesus as he grew up. The other one; we use to live together years ago "but **I KNOW** it's not him, because I don't want it to be him. Furthermore I have no idea where he is. I have not heard from him in fourteen. After that conversation; I could not get WT off my mind.

THE SHOCK OF MY LIFE

I thought of him uncontrollable. When I go to bed I would fall asleep thinking about him. When I wake; he was there in my thoughts. I would try to shake them. I would find myself talking to my customers about him. Some of them remembered him. Finally I shouted out to the Lord; **"Lord I don't know why this man is on my mind so heavy; but I know you know why; and you know where he is. "What ever the reason might be; please put me on his mind the same way he is on mine; and maybe he will call; because I do not know how to get in touch with him, it has been a long time.** I don't remember how long it took for that prayer to be answered; Sister Girl said; "it was two weeks later". I was finishing up my last customer's hair, and the phone ring. I answered as always; God bless you, Margaret speaking. The person on the other end said; "God bless you; WT speaking". I almost drop the phone. I repeated his name with a question; I asked; WT? "He said yes; "did you forget WT? He did not know my husband had passed, but he said he had been thinking about me all day. He had just moved into an apartment and was trying to un-pack some boxes; but could not get his mind off me. He stopped what he was doing; and got his old address book and decided to call. He said; "if my husband answered, he would say he was just thinking about the two of us and thought he would call and say hello".

I told him that I was almost finished with my last customer. I asked if he could call me back in about forty five minutes. So he did. We talked for hours. I told him that my husband was deceased. I asked if he had given his life to the Lord. He said yes; "God has a way of getting our attention". He said; "my Nephew committed suicide, one brother was dying with cancer, his only sister has had a mastectomy, and his oldest brother was an alcoholic; and the alcohol was killing him.

GETTING ENGAGED

We talked about how that if we had hooked up back fourteen years ago; it would not have worked out; because we were both still unstable. We got engaged that night before that conversation ended. WT said he would like to come visit that week end. We both agreed; but I received a call from my cousin that her son had been murdered. I needed to go to her. She was my little sister. I called WT back and explained what had happened. I told him my number seven child was going down with me and that we could stop to see him on our way back.

I started out driving first. We pulled into a rest area to sleep; I was too excited to fall asleep. When we reached my cousin's house and told them the news; they were happy too. WT had given me directions how to get to where he lived. When we got to his place; he took us out to the Farm where his Sister and her husband lived. Meeting them was like a breath of fresh air, and it's been that way with them ever since. They owned their own farm and breaded horses and participated in horse racing until they retired, and sold the farm. Every one that knows or have met them loves them. They are such an inspiration in our lives.

32.

Breaking the news About the wedding

WE BROKE THE NEWS to them of our engagement. They were shocked; they knew about his temper; but did not warn me. A friend of his mother; hinted a little something. I had no idea what she was trying to tell me. His Sister seemed happy. I had met her and some of WT's family fourteen years before. I also had met his Mother before she died. We set the date and six months later we were counseled by my Pastor. After the counseling; my Pastor said; "there was no doubt in his mind that WT was my mate" and he performed our wedding. He really sealed our Marriage. He spoke the blessing from Deuteronomy 28 over our lives. He gave us Communion and prayed the word over us, and blessed us. He even explained the meaning of the wedding bands in such great details. We married on Child number six's birthday. (All my children were in the wedding. Mickey gave me away.

THE WEDDING

Sister Girl and the Teacher was my Matrons-of-Honor, my Mama Sweet was escorted in as my mother. All of my X's family participated in my wedding. One Sister was my coronate; the other Sister took care of the money tree. One of the Nephews used my X's video camera to video the wedding. One Nephew and my Daughter sang; you Are so Beautiful, and Two Hearts, by Lionel Richie

We did not have a Honey Moon. My oldest daughter and husband treated us to a hotel suite. That was the most horrible wedding night of my life. I had waited four years far love making. Nothing happen. Things started going down hill immediately after we were married.

MOVING TO WT's HOME TOWN AND–RECEIVING HIS SON

We moved back to his home town. WT had told me that he did not have any bills and that I would not have to work unless I wanted to. Not only was he swimming in debt, but his credit was bad. He was employed as a police officer for eight years and didn't have eye water to cry with. We had a hard time finding an apartment. Finally we found a beautiful complex and found favor with the manager who rented to us. It was a three bedroom condo, with a fire place. We had not gotten settled in good before his son's mother called us and told us that Jr. was on the bus. She did not communicate with us about anything; just that he is on the bus, and to pick him up at the station. She told us what time he would arrive. That was the baby we broke up about years back. Jr. was fourteen when he came to live with us. Her plan was to cause problems; but just the opposite happened; we were like Mother and Son. He was a good kid which spoke well of her. He had been with her most of his years; sometimes with his Dad. She had raised a good mannerable Son. We got him in school; he got good grades, and got on the foot ball team. We would go to all his games and whatever school functions he had. Having him around made me youthful again. Later he ran track and won metals

I had rented my house discharged all my Clients. I had to go to one of the department stores to get a job in a Salon there. With my experience I was hired on the spot. It was another one of those times of building up my clientele. It was very slow. There were six of us operators building up our clientele. I was not making hardly any Money. I felt as though I was an added burden on WT. That gave me low self esteem. That is why it always pays to tell the truth. If I had known about the debt he had, we could have waited to get married, or not even do it at all. Things were getting real bad and we were not intimate at all.

LOOK AT THE GUN POINTED

One night I was in the room talking on the phone to my baby daughter. WT was ease dropping at the door. He thought he heard me say that I was going to leave him. When I got off the phone; and went into our bed room to get ready for bed; he went crazy. He beat me up, and pulled a gun on me. I thought I was gone! His son heard the commotion and came running in the bedroom to see what was happening. Jr. was already calling me Ma. He did not like what he saw. He said; "it reminded him of some things that had happened between WT and his Mom.

When WT went to work that next morning, I call my kids and told them what had happen; Knee Baby said; "get out of there right away". WT had called back from work to apologize. I acted as though it was forgotten. When I hung up the phone; Jr. and I packed that Buick and I was on the highway. I still had the Riviera. Knee Baby had rented the house for me, and the Tenant was still living in the house; so I moved in with her and husband. He was a great Son-in-Law.

The young man whom she had rented the house to; had heard that I was back; he was willing to break the lease if it was ok with me. I wanted my house back, so that was a blessing; we broke the lease, and I moved back into my house. Thanksgiving was just a few weeks away. WT had been calling; he talked me into letting him and Jr. spend that day with us. I had not moved into the house before thanksgiving. I agreed for them to come without consulting the children. Knee Baby's-husband thought that was a bad idea. He felt that I needed to end that relationship because a gun was involved. For some reason I Just could not end it yet.

33.

Getting back together

WHILE WT AND JR. were visiting; we talked about us getting back together; and that he would leave his job of eight years as a Police officer. He said; "he would do whatever it takes to be reconciled". I agreed because I loved him. I knew WT would have no problem finding work– Getting a job was like eating a piece of cake for him. WT would get hired wherever he applied; and with good pay. The love making was still next to none. I felt as if I was being punished by God; because I had been so permissive in my younger years. Everything else was pretty cool with him. He knew how to make me feel special. We moved into the house. He did get a good paying job as a supervisor at an Oil refinery. He worked there almost a year. He didn't like that one. He left that job and got another job at a nuclear plant. Every where he worked he would be hired in as Supervisor. But WT felt unsecured there. He soon moved on to another Site hired in as Supervisor.

It took thirteen years to find a finance Company to give me a loan to fix the roof in the Beauty Shop. It took them nine months to ok the Loan. The young man who was working with me had tried just about every Loan Company in the State before he found one. The interest rates were ski high; but I needed that roof fixed. Some one told me about a Minister name Rev. J. He was a roofer. I called him; and he promised me that it would not leak again. He and his crew did that roof and he was right. It never leaked again. Later I was able to get it re-financed at a little lower rate. WT and I soon paid it in full.

CUTTING UP MY COATS

We had an argument about sex one morning, I got up and got dressed and left the house. While I was gone WT cut up every coat, sweater, and jackets, even my real and fake furs. Knee Baby had given me her Monkey coat because her husband thought it was too flashy for her. That coat drew lots of attention. He cut it too. It was days before Jr. and I saw what he had done. We saw pieces of fur flying all over his bedroom for days. My coats hung in Junior's closet. We decided to investigate further to see where is this fur coming from; that's when we found the mess. I was devastated. This man– has cut every– coat and sweater I owned. WT had a friend whose girl friend's Mother lived in the City and she made, and mended coats. I called and made an appointment. She was an elderly Lady; full of wisdom. She really talked about WT. She talked about him and shared wisdom with him. She really made him feel about the size of a flea. He had to pay to get them all mended. She was great. You could not tell they had been cut. She did them all by hand. One coat was a long white wool Chester-field double breasted coat. She em-broaded that cut, and gave it a whole new look.

THE BEAUTIFUL HOUSE

A year later I got a divorce; I felt I had had enough. I was not ready to give up on the intimacy part of life. I thought I was ready to move on.

I had written down the type of house I wanted for us before the divorce. I had prayed over it and confessed on it. We had been divorced four months when I saw the house. It was minutes after it had been placed on the market. I had passed the house about twenty minutes before as I was going to the store. The sign was not in the yard the first time I went by. I was lead very strongly to come back that same way. Normally, I would never go that way to that– store. The sign had just been placed in the yard. I stopped in the middle of the street and yelled- **OH God;** I would love– to have that house" right away the devil said, "You know you can't afford that house". At first I accepted that lie, and then I remembered that he is the daddy of lies. Whatever the devil says–; just do the opposite of what he said. If he says go to the left–that mean go to your right–he's a layer

WT lived in an apartment across town, but we had not stopped talking to each other. He was showing me with gifts, coming over cutting the lawn, and picking up his mail. Just being the gentleman he should have been all the time; especially the gifts. I soon forgot about why we were divorced. We are so forgiving to each other. I soon forget how you treat me to the extent– of not trying to get even

One Sunday night Maggie and I had gone to the City, and we were a little late getting home. WT had been calling both our houses. He knew we were together–or she would know where I was; because she always stayed close to me. I took her home first; he reached her by phone first. By the time I was walking into my house; he was on the phone. I told him that he had mail. He came right over to get it. I told him about the house I had seen and asked him to stop by on his way back to look at it.

That Monday I woke up with the idea that we should go to the Credit Bureau and see what our credit report looks like. I called him and suggested that we go check it out, he agreed. When we returned to his apartment; he invited me in and suggested that he call the Realty to see if we might be able to see the house. The Realty said; "how about 45 min". That was great timing.

When I stepped in side the foyer, I could not close my mouth. The house had every thing I had written down months before. I mean exactly everything! First we had to see if we qualified to apply for the loan. We made an appointment and went to the office. The mortgage company checked us out and said– you are more than qualified. I knew then that had to be God answering my prayer because; our credit was jacked up; and we were not making that much money. WT had left the nuclear plant. He was working security waiting to be called to the Casino. He was still supervisor; but they were not paying a big salary. I was only working Three days a week in my salon. That was all I choose to work for the life of my business. And older Beautician had shared with me that kind of work would kill you if you did not use wisdom. She said her sister would sit on a stool and work long hours in the Beauty Shop. When she got ill; her customers would say to her–when you do me–you should go lay down" (when you do me) I took heed to her warning.

Re—married

The house was an older solid brick on a corner lot with a full finished basement with a wet bar. It was loaded. It had fourteen rooms. It was selling for one hundred and thirty thousand. The closets were full rooms with racks like a store. It also had a nice size sunroom. Everything I had asked for was there.

We explained our current situation to our Realty; he suggested we re-marry. So we re-married and got busy. We went to another town to re-marry so that it would not show up in our paper. It took us nine months to nail that deal. Satin got busy; don't ever think he is going to sit back and let a good thing take place without trying to stop it. Most of it we brought on ourselves. We had a lot of leg work and proof of payments on things that were negative on our credit report. The seller was not in any hurry. They never question why it was taking so long to close on the house. The people who had owned the house; the husband worked for a Company that transferred them to another state; and that Company had purchased the house, and we were purchasing it from them.

Just before my birthday in February we moved in. The cold weather held up until after the move. The house had both electric and gas hook up. But I hate electric cooking. Maggie got the Girls together and purchased for me a new gas stove with the waste-high broiler and automatic oven for my Birthday. We rented the other house again and made Maggie to over-see it. That April WT got hired at the Casino as Supervisor. He and I got into church, where he was working faithfully. He was head security guard, parking lot attendant; head usher, sang in the praise team, and the Pastor's Armor- Barer. His life was busy; but still fighting that habit which was controlling him. I spoke to the Pastor about the habit, hoping they would pray for him and offer some type of deliverance; instead they set him down and took everything away that he loved and enjoyed very much. WT and Maggie both got offended very badly and spiritually hurt, they both became inactive in any church for a long time. Maggie never joined another church.

About a Year later WT and I united with a church in another city. It was too large to really get involved into any of the miniseries. I think because we were not held accountable to any Ministry; strife entered in between us again. I went to the Pastor for help; but he blamed me for everything and made excuses for WT because he had served in the Army. In order to make an appointment with him; you had to tell the Secretary all your business before she thought you needed an appointment with the Pastor. I knew no place else to turn. I did pray; but we all have a will. No one can change you, but you. The threats started again, the gun threats, Jr. had graduated from High school and got a job at one of the fast food restaurants. He had gotten a little mouthy like talking back. WT went to his job and threatened him with the gun. He had to go to court. While WT was in court for that incident; Jebez, Mickey, and I were in the same court room to apply for an order of protection against him for threaten me with a gun too. The police came to our home and took the guns, but the Judge ordered them back to him because he had a permit. WT could use that ex-police story and get out of everything. The order of protection was granted to me. WT arrived home first from the court house. The boys went home with me, when we got home the sun room looked as if a tornado had hit it. WT had torn up all of our wedding pictures before moving out. Sister Girl's husband is photography and he gave me a deal on the price of the photos for only two hundred and fifty dollars. He destroyed them all.

WT was gone a few days and he started calling. Jr. was living with some friends, he was afraid to come back home. I kept reminding WT he was breaking the law by calling; but he kept calling. I gave in and he came back home.

Our living room was still empty for two years. One Thursday night before I went to bed; I walked into the living room and said– I command you to be filled with furniture– in the Name of Jesus". And I went to bed.

That next day was my Friend who owned the Comb's birthday. I called her to sing happy birthday to her and to ask what she had planned to do. She said; "we are going to the Boat". "I said I may join you". I went to work; my last customer for the evening was a Casino Host at the Boat. I told her that I had planed to go on the Boat, but I was too tired to go. She always called me Mom. She said, "You're going; "just put some jell on my head and stick me under the dryer". Go home put on your high heal shoes like you always do; and I am going to call and make reservations for you". "You will not have to pay for parking". I could not back out after that order; I did just that.

When I got to the Boat; there were not any machines open. It's Friday night; everybody was on the boat. I walked around not really caring if any machines became vacant. I looked for my friend finally I saw her; but I did not want to stand around her. So I moved on. Finally a lady got up from the Home Run machine. I sat down; I only took sixty dollars to play with. I had played about an hour. I had played forty dollars and ask the host to give me coins for the last twenty. I played for about twenty minutes more; and the machine sounded off. I did not know what was happening. The lady sitting next to me said; "you have hit Home Run". I said what is that? She said you have won five thousand dollars; look up there—see the figures. I could not believe what I was seeing.

They took out the taxes and paid me my money with cash. The Lady asks me if I had anything to put the money in. I said no; she asks if I had on socks, and I did. She gave me a safety pin and told me to go into the bath room, take off my socks, put the money in it and pin it to my bra. I thanked her and went and did what she suggested. WT was still employed there and was he was just coming to work. He worked mid-nights. Some one had told him his wife had won. He met me at the landing and asks was it true. I said yes; he said; "you are kidding". I said; no I am not kidding. He escorted me home; and he went back to work.

I paid my tithes first. Knee Baby and I went to the furniture store and purchased everything I wanted for my living room. We even found a store that sold name brand furniture for half the price of the big expensive stores. If you did not see what you had in mind; they would order what ever you wanted from their catalog. So that completed the furnishing for my big beautiful house.

After I paid my tithes; my pastor where I was a member at that time; said; I could not work in his church; because I had gone to the Boat. He did not give the tithes back that came from the boat. I should have asked him to give my money back. (Just Joking)

34.

WT Got Fired

THINGS WENT WELL FOR about seven years; then all hell broke loose again. We always celebrate every body's birthdays and Holidays. That was my way of keeping the family together. It was number four's birthday. WT had been fussing and cursing for a few days. He had gotten fired from his job. He was very angry at the world; because some people on the job lied about an altercation that had taken place as he and some other guards had to subdue a drunken customer and put him off the boat. WT had received all kinds of awards for outstanding performances every year of the five years he worked there. He knew his job and did it well. He could write the most detail report. When ever an incidents; would occur on the job; he could write the report so accurate; it was as if you were there. His Manager liked that, because most of his Guards could not write good reports. He even covered for his Manager when he was goofing off, and he did that a lot. I'm from old school– you do not ever have your bosses, or Managers coming to your home. I had shared that with WT. He would invite him any-way. They would drink wine and shoot the bull. He would even bring wine with him some times. He was already afraid that WT wanted his job. When he first applied for the job at the Casino; he was told that he was being hired in as Manager. But the person who interviewed WT got ill before he was to report on duty. Whoever stepped up in his place hired him in as Supervisor instead of Manager. He and the Manager got tight; but he was always afraid that WT was out to get him because He knew his

176

job. He was sharp, and was always prompt and on time. His Manager wouldn't even speak up in his behalf. Every one who conspired to get him fired; also got fired some months later; even the Manager.

WT found a job driving Limousine for some company paying peanuts. People would be drinking and giving him a hard time. At the party that Sunday; he was so angry with every one. WT thought everybody was plotting against him. Knee Baby was his favorite, but she could not calm him down. He threatens me and speed off. The kids thought I should leave the house. So I did; I went to spend a day or so with Baby daughter and her husband, but because of their relationship, I did not feel too comfortable there. I call my lawyer and filed for an Order of protection so I could go home. He was ordered out of the house while I was still away. WT said; "he was sleeping because of the crazy shift he was working. When the police ring the door bell and told him he had to leave the house; he was shocked because he had not done anything; and had no place to go; and no money to get there. He had called me to see where I was. I knew that WT was only a big bag of win and that I had no need to leave. His anger never last but a few minutes, but because nobody could not talk to him; the kids thought I should not be there when he return. His bluff; was threatening me with a gun. That was too much bluffing for me. I was tire of the guns. My thing about guns is; they are to be used; not try to scare anybody with them. They are not a toy. We were already loosing the house because he had been fired. Age was becoming a factor of finding good paying jobs.

Any man gets frustrated when he feels that he can't support his family. WT is a man loaded with pride. There are many times we could have avoided many problems if we could talk when he is angry. Talking makes him angry. I always say it takes a special Man to go to Viet-Nam twice–and it takes a special woman to love him. I packed his things and put them in the garage. He hired our neighbor to take them to the storage. A week later; WT left town and I had to find a place to move. I gave lots of furniture away. People were passing. And I was calling them in and giving it away. The house of my dreams had gone into foreclosure. I really hated loosing the house and my Marriage. WT was too angry to talk to me. Proverbs 12:15 say; "a fool thinks he needs no advice, but a wise man listens to others". A wise man knows that anger causes mistakes. We have made many of them in this marriage. My Grand-Pa use to quote that scripture; anger lies in the bosom of a fool.

35.

Finding a place to move

I HAVE MANY PLAY daughters. One of them Lanett and her husband looked out for me. Her mother and I became good friends when we were in the Club. Her mother's club would invite our club to her City to their annual affairs every year. When she got ill, she gave me a ring as keep sake. Lanett had been a care giver for an elderly lady. When the Lady died; she willed a two bed room brick house with a full basement to her. The house was empty at the time I needed a place to move. They gave me permission to live there temporally until the tenants in my house could move out. Ray moved me mostly all by herself in her huge van. Lanet was putting the house on the market in a few months. She gave me first choice to purchase the house. She let me move in and pay them only what I could afford. The tenants who were living in my house were supposed to be looking for a place to move. Ray had told Lanett that they were going to purchase the house for me. So I was not in any hurry for the tenants to move out until the deal of purchasing the house fell through. I let them know that I needed the house soon. I would check with them daily to hear about their progress.

It took the tenants from October to April; and they still had not found a place to move. I had to get busy and find a place for them to move. Lanett had a buyer for the house. The closing date was just days away. I had to find some one to move me, and I only had very little money to pay a mover. WT had all the utilities turned off at our house when he left. Winter was approaching; I needed the utilities on I had to put a deposit on everything in order to have them put in my name.

I went to my neighbor; the same ones who moved WT. He and his wife were also our friends; I explained my situation to both of them together. Moving was his part time job. He and his wife agreed to move me for the price I offered to pay. We all had gone to dinner from time to time. She and I would cry on each others shoulders over a cup of coffee. We were that kind of friend.

I helped the tenant find a place to move. She was a single Mother with two children and a live in boy friend on section 8. He was too sorry to find a place for them to move. When I talked to her the day before; she promised; they would be out in plenty time for me to move in. Mickey and his cousin came to help load the truck. His Cousin brought his girl friend with him and some things disappeared along with my white Chester field coat. When we loaded up everything, and got to my house; the people were still in the house. She and her mother were moving in a pick up truck. My stuff had to stay on the truck over night. I ask the mover if that would be a problem. He said no; "it would be no problem; he did not have any business schedule for the next day". We did not discuss any additional charge. If it had been a problem; my hands were tied; because I had no more money. I looked at it as another blessing from God. I was under the impression that since he knew my situation; everything would be ok with the furniture having to stay on the truck over-night; or at least discussed an amount it would cost instead of waiting until they unloaded the truck. Things had changed from the original plan without me knowing it.

The next day Mickey and Jebez helped unload the truck. When we were all finished, I was amazed at the price; it was too much; I could not pay it. All I had was what we agreed upon at first. Some day I hope to pay that balance. It seemed to have nullified our friendships. I talk to his wife later; her reply was "I don't know what you and my husband's arrangements were". I did not know how to take that comment. I went away sad, because I had set him straight years before I ever met her. I really did treasure her friendship. I never get the chance to let friendships go; they are the ones to let me go and I never know why. We did not have time to clean the house before moving in. When I got all moved in; the floors were so nasty and roaches were every where. My

Son-in-Law piled all the furniture in one room at a time, and he and Ray purchased new carpet and hired some one to help him pull up the old dirty carpet, and put down the new, and painted the walls. I used Borax acid to get rid of the bugs; it got rid of them all very quickly. The house was like new.

WT and I were talking again. I had promised him that I was not getting a divorce this time, but circumstances changed everything; I had no choice. I had reached the age to draw Social Security. I didn't want another divorce, but the system says you can not draw Soc; Sec from a deceased mate if you are married. The rule is you can marry whomever you want after the divorce. A year later we were re-married. We have married each other three times. I told Pastor; I truly believe in words we speak. The Bible tells us; we can speak life or death. We choose life. He really sealed our marriage. No matter what we've done to each other, forgiving comes so easy for both of us. We do not dwell on the past.

Maggie berried herself into her Daycare. She had developed breast cancer and hid it from us until she got ill. She was afraid to go to the Doctor until it was too late. She contracted pneumonia and we took her to the hospital; the Nurses and the Doctor thought she had had a Mastectomy. They ask why she didn't take care of that cancer sooner. She really did suffer with lots of Pain. I never saw anything as ugly as that Cancer was. To look at it would make you know she was suffering. I suffered with her. She kept saying she did not have insurance. She was a very stubborn young lady. If she set her mind to something; you could not change it. I could go to her for any Business advice. She was a family child. She always knew what I needed and would contact the other siblings to get it done. We talked every day.

36.

Selling the house

THE HOUSE HAD BECOME a burden. I could not get the necessary funds to do any repairs. I had moved one of my grand-daughter in with me temporarily, however, it turned out not be temporarily. These young people don't think maturely; and arrangement was becoming too much to handle. I was talking to the Lord asking Him about what I should do about my situation. He spoke to my spirit; and said, "Sell the house. Ask what you think it is worth, and set your selling date". I set the date for one month from that date which was my birthday. I also set the price. I called my realty and sign the papers. He only showed the house twice and it sold one month from that date, and sold for my asking price and the buyer never negotiated. I went out and help my grand-daughter find her an apartment while I was waiting for my closing date; the question came up about where I was going to move. I really did not know where. I heard that voice say speak to me again. I thought it was the Holy Spirit that said I could move down with WT. He said he already was established in his apartment, and I would not have to worry about paying rent, or utilities. But I did not mention it to him; because when a thing involves two or more people; the Spirit will tell them also, what he has told you. I wasn't sure it was God at that time. So I waited.

WT and I were on the phone talking one evening and I was telling him that I had put the house on the market and I had a buyer. He asked where I was going to go. I said, right now; I don't know. He said to me exactly what the Holy Sprit had spoken to me, about moving in with him. I knew that was a confirmation. The Holy Spirit also said; do not tell your children yet. Some of them will not under stand because of what you been through with WT, especially Maggie. He said; "they will not under stand that this is my doing". I began to put things in storage; she found out about what I was doing; and she really did not want me to go back with WT. She felt that I deserved better. She cried and called other members of the family to talk me out of it. My oldest grand son called from Virginia; giving his advice; Ann called; and call herself telling me off. She became my- Mama. I could not get a word in between her breath. I began to wonder if she was taking a breath. I ended the conversation by hanging up on her. I had heard from God. It hurt me to hurt my sick child; because I knew she did not have long to live. But we must always obey God to receive His blessings. God had already prepared me. The cancer had eaten away her lungs. She passed while I was in the process of moving. That halted the move for a while. I really felt like an out sider. Some one had come in and taken lots of her stuff. I had no say about anything. My Daughters probably is not aware of it; but when something is happening in our family. I become on the out side of the situation.

Their Father died a year before Maggie. She really never got over our divorce. She always hoped that we would get back together. We almost did five years after our divorce. We had set the date for our getting back together. I thought he was already married; but there was no mention of him having to get a divorce in order for us to get back together. Then there was no more communication from him about our getting back together. Years passed before I found out why. I was told that his brother; the Pastor had talked him out of us re-marring. He told Jahari the lady he was with would not be able to take it; if he left her. That was ok: except I should have been told; because he came to me with the idea. I would have understood; because I had reservations about it any way

MAGGIE LEAVING US

Maggie was a daddy's child. She was a loving Daughter; but she did not learn how to let things go. Holding on to hurts will do the same to your body; as bad food, and the same as not being able to forgive. I begged her to go to the Doctor. She asked her girl friend who she grew up with; and were like Sisters all through collage not to tell us. I never could under stand that kind of friend.

She was never married. She had a son; she always said; if whoever she meets could not be a father figure to her son; she would never marry just to say she had a man. She was a stern mother. She was on his case, and he could not get away with much. She had a paddle made with a hole in it. When she needed to whip that butt; He would come running to Grand-ma for protection. Some times I could talk her down, but I did not want to spoil him. He was grown when she left us. She was the back-bone of the family. She just wanted everything to be right for her family, but neglecting herself. She always looked out for me. She knew what I felt without me telling her. Even as they were growing up, she would always tell her siblings; you know Mama told you not to do that. Everybody else came before herself. She was the only one who went right out of high school to collage. She helped me to get through Beauty School. She went to work for the Government, and had a house built from the ground for her and her son. She had such great imaginations especially about a house. All the girls do have that. She was also a great budgeter. She did not buy a lot of clothes; but her son had every thing he needed accept his father. She left that job to come live near her Mom she was so family oriented.

We have not been able to make her son understand that God did not take his Mother. Jesus came that we may have life, and to have it more abundley. Satin comes to rob, steel, and to kill. She had the responsibility to watch out after her own body as we all do. Her stubbiness took her from us. We miss her terribly. Children were never meant to leave the parents.

Auto Accident

I put my furniture in storage in Illinois and I moved in with him on A Friday. We got married at his sister's home that next Friday. Their pastor remarried us. We started looking for a church. Bill and I had visited one on Key Stone a few times. WT could not go one Sunday; he had to work, so I went along. I was driving up Kessler in the right lane; a car was stopped, and was turning from my left lane, I was going straight. A Lady coming the opposite direction, turned in front of me and hit my car, the air bag exploded. I passed out and hit a tree at the intersection. When I came to myself a man was helping me from the car, and helped me set on the curve. The Lady kept saying; "she hit me". The police could see what had happen. She got the ticket. I had been sitting on the curve a while before I realized that my wig was not on my head. The impact had knocked it off. I always wore it pretty tight, but it was behind the seat on the floor. The ambulance came. I had already called WT and he was there licitly-split. He and the ambulance were there at the same time. WT told them which Hospital I was to be taken to. I had a broken arm I was so blesses that God spared me; because trees don't move.

My car was totaled. It was a beautiful Park Avenue with green metallic bottom and beige top. People would be stopped at the light and say to me; "what a beautiful car. It had been a one owner. Louise had paid it off for me before I moved. The Insurance paid enough money to purchase another one; same year. A Buick La saber Brown and Beige. I have never seen another Park Avenue with that same color. It had been special ordered by the owner.

THE NEW HOUSE

A year from the foreclosure we began to look at houses. Realtors would say; "you must wait three years before you are eligible to purchase a house because of the foreclosure". I would say, Thank you, but that is not what God said. We kept looking. We realized that was the law, but every thing is based on what God has to say. He has already given us Spiritual blessings. All we need is faith, and I had that. WT was working at a Resort Site he was Supervisor there too. One afternoon He was on his way from work when he heard an advertisement about a new subdivision being built. He told me about it, and said do you think we should check it out? I said, by all means; we must check out all possibilities.

We called and made an appointment for that following Sunday. They sent us to see three of their models. The one I liked was also in another subdivision. The salesman said, "You seem to be one who likes a quieter area". I said I do. He sent us over to see the other house. Some one else had had a loan on that house, but it did not go through. As a matter of fact they had the house built for themselves. We went back to the office and filled out the papers and got approved. I was so happy to move into a brand new house in a quite neighborhood. We were the first to live in it. By the time our three years were up; we had already lived in the house a year. I had faith and God did it for us. Faith moves God's hand in our lives.

We had very nice neighbors. I even tried to start up a young adult class for the girls in that area. They attended for a while but soon stop coming. One of the girl's, Mother had died the first year we moved there. The other girl's Mother had three daughters; and was a single parent. She was so disappointed when her girls stopped, because she could see that they were getting out of hand. She was so happy that somebody wanted to help, but they stop attending.

LOOSING MY SECOND MOM!

I got the call that Mama Sweet was getting ready to make her transition. I went to be by her side. When ever anything would go wrong with her; my Sisters would always call me. I loved that in them. She and I were so close. When ever she wanted to go shopping; she would call me and off we would go to the Mall. She would buy something for herself, and me too if I would agree. She just loved me that much. Some Mondays and Saturdays I would call and say get ready. I have to go to the City to purchase supplies. She would say give me time to find something to put on. We would set an approximate time as to how long it would take her to get dressed and off we'd go. We hung out all the time. She loved to go to O C B. We would go early afternoons when there were less people there, because her hands shook and she still had her pride even in her nineties. We would find us a corner booth all by ourselves. We both loved their bread pudding. Mama and I were both of the same sign. We would always confess that we did not ever want to have to live with any one, or live in a home. God answered her prayer. I believe him to answer mine; I really miss her. We use to laugh and say; her son was jealous of our relationship. He would tell her;☺ "you can eat a hundred pound of Mag's mess, and ask the doctor if another hundred pounds will hurt. Mr. D knew his family and I were close. The only times his Dad would allow him to use his auto; was if it would benefit me and the Children.

HAVING MY SURGERIES

I had retired from Cosmetology after thirty three years; because my right knee, and back had almost stop working. I went to therapy for months. I even had the cortisone shots in my knee but to no avail. He said I needed to go see an Orthopedic Surgeon to see what he recommends. He sent me to his friend. He said he is a Christian too. I made the appointment with the Surgeon; and he did recommend surgery. He sent my husband and me to watch a video; to show us instructions on what type of exercises to do and not to do after the surgery, especially if you have back problems. I had the knee replacement December twenty second; I came home from the Hospital on Christmas day.

The Therapist came to my home for six weeks. I forgot what I had learned from the video. I did not tell the Therapist that I had back problems. After those six weeks was over I could barely walk. Those exercises threw my back out. I was starting to feel less pain walking bent over. I could not see me walking bent over; so four months later In April; I had the back surgery. My Baby Daughter and her husband came to be with me and to pray with me before I went with the Surgeon. After surgery, I was great they went back to Illinois When I went home she came back to take care of me for a week. I was doing so well; I no longer needed her. When she left; WT was my nurse. When he got home from work he would cook. He made sure my ice was in tact, and that I was comfortable. He was a good nurse and took very good care of me and the dog. We had a Pomeranian dog. She was my company until he gets home from work. She knew what time he should be coming into the garage. She would go to the door every day at the same time to wait for him. When Jebez came around; she would cry to follow him.

Both doctors were amazed at my progress for my age. I only had to see the back Surgeon one visit after the Surgery. The healing process took place quickly because, we prayed right before the surgery; and I eat right, and exercise. I had been talking to him about it all a long before the surgery. It is a little different with the knee. They start out seeing you the first its six weeks, three months, six months, one year, then every two years. I'm now in the every two years. I am pain free. I was able to get back into my high heal shoes. I am not dressed without them. Glo said if I precede her in death; she will put a high heel shoe on my Casket. (That's funny)

THE BREAK UP

After I got back on my feet, in the summer WT enjoyed working in the yard. We had a beautiful yard. We won the most beautiful lawn contest one year. I was doing an in home business. WT started acting strange. We never knew why but he got transferred to another site. He still had his level of good workmanship; always did his work well. Spending twenty years in the military would probably be a habit hard to break; being a supervisor sometimes he would talk to his employers a little too demanding. I came to that conclusion because that is the way he comes cross to me. If you ask him a question, he would answer as if that was a dumb question. I would tell him the only dumb question is a question un-asked. I warned him a lot about that tone of voice. After working at that site a few months; he was transferred to a down town site where all kind of action was happening, good and bad. A tornado hit the down town one weekend. The building WT worked in got hit pretty badly. He became so obsessed with working down there; he began to call it his building. Every where we went; that was his whole conversation. It seems he was going off the deep end. That is where it all started. He began to have confrontations with his bosses. He said; "everybody was against him". He would talk to himself, get angry and throw things. Then he started in on me. I could not do anything right. He had stop eating at home. He was working nights and not sleeping. He lost forty pounds in such a short time. He was acting as if he was on drugs. Family members on both sides were very concern.

He stops paying any of the bills, and the threats started in again. He pulled the gun on me again; and was spending money for everything except what was needed. We began to get notices about the house payments and the utilities. I had a credit card so I began to pay the utilities. He got angry about everything I did. After he threatens me with the gun, I called the police, but he had left by the time they arrived.

I then call the abuse hotline. The agent met me in a near by restaurant. They don't come to your house. I was trying to see if she could give me any pointers on how to deal with the situation. I thought he was ill. I had never seen him act like he was acting before. He saw the car parked in front of the restaurant; so he rushed in and started loud talking, so the agent called the Police. I think he thought he would find me with a man. He was gone again by the time they arrived. The Agent suggested I go to a Shelter. I was escorted to the house by the police, WT was not there. I got a few clothes, and she signed me into the Shelter. I felt so out of place. I felt like that was another one of those times I acted on someone else's advice. I went, but I only stayed one night. There were no beds available. The surgery was still new. A very nice lady who was there let me sleep on the couch. She said; "I can not let you sleep on that hard floor". I thanked her. When I left; she walked me to my car, we exchanged information. I gave her my cell phone number but I never heard from her.

I went to Illinois where my children were. WT did not know where I was. He called me on my cell and said that we needed to talk. I told him I was in Illinois; he drove to Illinois where I was at Knee Baby's house. After the talk, we decided that we should go our separate ways. I went back home and began to pack. When I would go to bed he would unpack some boxes to take out what he thought would benefit me. He had told me to take what I wanted. He had too much pride to ask me not to go, and I hade too much to stay. Pride comes before a fall. We both fell hard. I filed for another order of protection because of the gun. But I was not going to appear at court against him. I was moving back to Illinois.

I rented a twenty six foot truck and the kids came to help pack the truck. We had to call the police again. He was angry with everybody; and threading to shoot everybody. The Police took the gun until we left. He had a permit for it, but not to threaten people with it. He and Mickey got into it because Mickey asked him if he may have his Bicycle. We had had the bikes ten years and never rode them. He did not stay angry with Mickey very long, the kids love WT, and he loves them. He has been in their lives from 1968 to 1977 then again from 1988 to the present.

I moved into one of Ann's houses. She was into Real Estate. One of her houses was empty and had been empty for some time, as if it was waiting for me, and she let me move in. I could not pay her any rent. I was told by one of my play daughters, that I was eligible for one month rent, so I applied and did received a check. Ann let me keep it to help me get on my feet. She is such a giver. I would go over to her house to help her out with my G G's as she is raising her five grand children.

Mondays were laundry; and cook day. Tuesday was Iron the kids clothes day, and cook. I would cook every day for my G, G'S. (great grand's) She released me to go to work doing in-home care.

WT moved to Tenn. with his Son. Before he moved he had called and told me he was watching me. That was what caused me to follow through with the order of protection. I did not know what was going through his mind. As I said I had not ever seen him act so radical. I thought he was suffering from P.T.S. (Post Dramatics Syndrome.) I had told him I was not coming to court. But when he call and said that; I got scared. When he saw me in court, he was so angry; because he said I had lied to him about not coming to court; and he was so short tempered with the judge; she assigned a five year order of protection against him. My Lawyer said they had never heard of a five year order of protection before. That Judge was feeling my pain.

After he moved out of State; about six months Ann and I came back and lifted that order; because he could not even get a job with that over his head. I did not want to cripple his lively hood. My desire was to stay in Indiana, but I could not find a place to rent because of my income. So I had no other choice but to move back to Illinois.

It was a Friday night in December; two weeks before Christmas and four months after moving back; my house was broken into. I always kept a door jam under the door knob of the back door. When I unlocked the front door and saw my mattress hanging off the bed. I ran back out side and called 911. When the Police got there; I went back inside with them. The robbers had pride the hinges from the back door. The door jam was still in place. The Police said, "There had been four other homes broken into that night". He said; "they seem to be kids looking for small things such as Play Stations and electronic games". They took my potable file cabinet with all my personal files; a new Camcorder still in the box. They took several things that I missed later. I spent the next week canceling and reporting stuff that were missing. I saw the boys as I was walking to my car. There were about five of then all dressed in black. I thought nothing of it. If you don't have a criminal mine sometimes you will let your guard down. I went on to church.

About a month later; I forgot to lock my car one night; some one took all my CDs, and my bible. It was in a case that looked like a purse. I guess when they saw that it was not a purse they threw it away. I really missed my bible; it had years of marked scriptures in it, and was large print. I hope they found that one scripture that says; "**thou shall not steal**" The CDs were mostly Christian. I can never replace them. When some one goes into your private place; you feel so naked; so invaded

IN-HOME CLASSES

I took some classes for In-Home Care; they signed me to Mrs. Pat. She was such a sweet lady. We had such a bond. Even though she was Caucasian; our lives were so similar. She would always tell me she loves me, and I loved her too. I would help her with her bath and rub her down with warm oil and pray over her. She said that the pain in her body was almost gone. We would go to lunch together. She needed a wheel chair to go out of her apartment to the car. She loved for me to bring her some of what I cook. Her favorite food was fried okra. That's what she would order when we went to lunch. If they did not have any on the buffet, I would ask them to fix her an order. They were very nice about that. When I leave and go home I felt so fulfilled. I enjoy making people comfortable. Some times the Agent would call for me to go feed some one or take another one to the Doctor. They would not want me leave; because I have so much patient with elderly people. They didn't know why; but it was the Jesus shining through me. She was happy living on her own.

One Saturday she was feeling good enough to make her bed, and fell. She was taken to the hospital for observation, from there to rehab at a nursing facility. She never made it back to her apartment. I visited her often; sometimes my sons and daughter would go with me to visit her. She got to know Glo very well. When I walk in to see her, she would cry because I stayed in touch with her. She became my friend. Her daughter was very attentive to her. She always kept her medicine measured, and she would make sure I had what I needed to take good care of her Mother.

I had been praying for a chance to move back to Indiana before I took the class. When that door opened; I knew it was Him. When He opens a door for you; He has a way of letting you know it is Him; because God does not want anyone else to get the glory. I found a beautiful apartment with affordable rent; but if Mrs. Pat had not fallen, as much as I wanted to move back; I would have stayed to take care of her. She said I was like family to her. I felt the same by her. But after she left; my daughter told me she needed her house. They wanted me to move into an apartment in Illinois. They were too expensive. I could not pay the rent there. That <u>REALLY</u> was the answer to my prayers. Because of the income I earned from working; aided me to rent an apartment in the City where I wanted to live.

God gave me favor with the managers at a wonderful quiet complex and the people in charge are SPECTACKLER. I believe I am the apple of their eye. I really like it here. We believe God for another house. WT and I asked for forgiveness for loosing the other two. Most of the reason was job related, pride, and anger. That is why God say so much about pride and anger. But He is a forgiving God.

BACK TOGETHER

My Intention was to get a divorce after I moved back to Indiana. I even went to Legal Aid and paid the application fee to apply, but I had a waiting period because I had not lived back in the State long enough. Even though I had lived here before; I had been gone more than a year. It would have cost very little to get it. While waiting I was convicted by the Holy Spirit not to follow through, and not to get another divorce. I had peace with that. After two years of separation; both of us went through so much drama; at our age. When do we learn? So we are back together. I am happy I listened to that voice; because that same voice spoke to me after he was back; to make a Doctor's appointment for him. I did; and they found he had a prostate problem. The Doctor was able to catch it in time.

We are older now and realize it is time out for the stupid stuff. God really got our attention this time. All we have been through; it must be something there; I do not know what keep us going back and forth. Well– I love the man. He has a good heart, I'm a softy to. WT came into my life when my children were young; and when little Jebez needed some directions from a male. He treats my children as his own. He does more for them than I agree for him to do. When Jebez was living with us; He was blessed with a good paying job. We wanted to see him get on his feet. We are still waiting

We both are retired now. WT enjoys Golfing; and I like using the computer a lots; then we together do what we like. I am still working at home doing an in home base business. I have done just about every one out there. The one I'm doing now is really my nitch. It is something that makes women look good and feel better. Men wear them too. I enjoy my life. I have many gifts and talents.

THE SCAM

My up-line in the Business is my Niece. She met a person who told her about a man; who could really help our business grow fast. She had an interview with him. He said; "he was a Marketing Director. Three of us ladies fell for the scheme. He talked me into purchasing a credit card machine that would cause people who were not financially able to come into the business; could do a ninety day payment plan. If we give him the names of the customers; he would do the peeking, (or the sales pitch) and get them to come in. He really did sound legit. He comes in the name of a preacher. He would preach us a sermon when he called. He would tell me what he preached about that Sunday at his church. That is what he used to scam us with. When the machine arrived; it was nothing like what he had said. Let this be a lesson. If a person has to tell you they are a Christian; run as fast as you can.

I let him talk me into purchasing the machine. The contract was none cancelable. As we started processing my application they called back and said I was too old. That should have been a red flag for me. He asks if I had some one who would come on the application with me. I said my husband is younger than I am. He signed for me; but the business is in my name.

After I purchased the machine and finally got it working. I had two customers who each wrote a check for their merchandise; when I processed those two checks through that credit card machine; the company took part of the money from each check. Two other companies took money out of my account, plus monthly fees for the machine. I was only supposed to pay eighty nine, ninety nine a month for the machine. I sent the machine back, now the company is trying to make me pay four thousand dollars for the machine. This so call marketing director won't return our calls. He also sent a machine to my up-line in someone else's name and took money from her account. She went thought hell to get her money back. The last I heard from her she still had not received her money. Now this so call Marketing Director has the credit card machine. I suppose they are using it while I pay for it. I'm hoping this be a lesson for some one. When any thing sound too good to be true; than it most likely is. Since this happen to me; I have herd warnings over the TV about people using Christianity to scam people. That's how he got me. I was just not thinking. I never met the people. Never do business over the phone. You just might be talking to satin and his daughter.

I am free to do whatever I like. I only like to do well. My husband does not mind. We are in a good Church and we have some great friends here, and he and I talk more. Our dream is to travel. He said God whipped his butt good this time concerning that temper. He says he has learned that he can't change any one. That is God's job. We never get too old to change. I was told by him and his sister that his dad had a terrible temper. I met his sweet Mother, but his Father had died before I met him. As Christians we must strive to be like our heavenly Father. Some of our earthly parents may not make it into heaven. My kids Father told me before he died; that he did not have anything to ask me to forgive him for. I said ok; I dared not try to remind him. We remained friends until his death. He and his wife visited our house and we did like wise; and when her Son was small he stayed at our house most of the time. He calls me Ant Mag. Glo always looked after him. He was an only child too, and I under-stood his loneness.

I am not trying to say that I have no blame. Even-though I prayed not to be like my mother; I see some of her in me some times. I have a way of telling you off without using profanity. I soon remember what second Corinthian say; therefore, if anyone is in Christ, he is a new creation; the old has gone, the new has come. 1 john 4-17 says I am like Christ in this world. I never saw where He had a temper. He said be angry and sin not.

Jebez left us and moved to another State; and got married again He mixed with a wrong crowed and went to prison again. I was cool that time. I didn't let it freak me out because I had drawn a picture for him as to what could happen. I preached it over and over to him.

But what really almost caused me to freak out; was when he was released from prison; he almost went back to prison for something he did not do. His wife decided she'd had enough. They had been through quite a bit together. She had decided to brake up with him while he was in Prison. I did not blame her for that; and he needed some place to be parole to. She was nice enough to let him use her address, which was also his address before going to prison.

When he was released; he was on parole, and also on house arrest with a leg monitor. I was told; that his wife and some friends were out at a club; sitting in a car. Some one walked up to the car and shot and killed the man sitting in that car with them. They said Jebez did it. The only thing saved him was; his house arrest monitor had just been checked by the Authorities; and his two Step-Sons had seen him in bed when they went to the bath room about the same time the murder happen. We got in touch with his Parole Officer and requested him to be transferred to our address in Illinois.

He was so in love with her; the only way he knew how to love. He had never seen it in operation. We contacted his Parole Officer and requested he come home. He granted the request and put him on a Bus. After he was a home a few weeks; he started asking us if his wife could come too. Our house was small, after so much begging we agreed. I was not feeling her; but we ended up letting her come too. She came a few weeks later. A friend she knew also came to Illinois shortly after her. He moved in to a hotel room not too far from us. He seemed to be a nice fellow; but everyday he would come by the house and talk to her in private. Jebez would be upset, but he was cool. The next thing we heard the friend had committed suicide. That really shook her and her kids up. We did not blame Jebez for wanting his wife. She was his wife. They both lived with us a few months.

While they were living there; I began to love her like a daughter of mine. I felt real close to her. I wanted her to get into church; she said; "she did not have clothes for church" so I began to buy her clothes. She began to go to church with me. After a while they moved into an apartment.

The Lord gave me a real love for my daughter-in-law. Her Mother had died when she was young. Even today we have a great relationship. Her children are my grand children. She finally got a divorce.

Jebez says his desire always was to be a truck driver. We helped him get all of the credentials he needed to be one. He is a certified truck driver. Both Sons has struggled with the penal system. Their Father and I may have played role in that part of their lives. Parents need to take inventory in discovering the roots of their life styles and how much love is shown. In most cases, this means we have to examine our childhoods. What needs were not met there? What negative experiences or messages about ourselves did we absorb in the dysfunctional family of origin? A parent's pain or frustration is discharged against or projected onto the child. Passive abuse occurs when key elements are missing within the family. A child growing up needs fifteen to twenty years of consistent loving; from two sane sober relatively happy parents. A child requires time, attention, and affection. Anything, such as workaholic, that hinders or limits the parent's ability to give these things can result in passive abuse. Sometimes we parents inflict or play a part in our children's addictions. But when we grow up we must confront and assess the full extent of our dependencies. We all have some kind; if it's only chocolate. Smoking or sex

God has been so good to me his mercy endures forever. Through all the foolish things I have done. He has kept me. He who dwells in the shelter of the most high will rest in the shadow of the almighty. Ps 91:1 Love is Patient and kind. Love is not jealous or boastful or proud or rude. Love does not demand its own way. Love is not irritable, and it keeps no record of when it has been wronged. It is never glad about injustice but rejoices whenever the truth wins out. Love never gives up, never looses faith, is always hopeful, and endures through every circumstance. 1COR 13:4-7 Love heals everything. Love will heal my Sons, Grand Sons. I have plenty to give. I can't give up. A quote from one play daughter; "Minor set backs are major come ups"

This is my time to celebrate, I made it. I stop asking; why did I go through it. I thank God I was able to come through the out door toilets, the divorces, the abusive relationships. I stop judging myself and others. God loves us enough to love our dirt as he stoop down and wrote in the dirt and ask the woman; where are thy accusers? We go through the valleys, so we can get to the mountain. God can't use a man until he is broken. Abraham is known throughout the earth as a founder of a great nation, a portion of this greatness must be created to his wife, Sarah. 1peter3:6 tell us if we follow in Sarah's steps, we will do well. What did Sarah do that was so special? What makes her an example?

What makes her an example to follow? She was quite a remarkable girl, but she didn't start out that way. In fact it took her a long time to wise up! When she married Abe, her name was Sarai, meaning contentions and vicious," a real nag. Although she was the local beauty queen, she had no beauty within. Many years went by before she got the message that making a good marriage a great marriage would rest largely on her. God told her to submit to Abe. At least, she decided to adapt to his way of life. She began to grant his every desire, and he returned the favor! She started calling Abe lord it wasn't his idea, it was hers. This change of attitude caused God to change her name to Sarah, which means princess what a change —from vicious to princess. Their marriage started to sizzle when Sarah was ninety-nine! And isn't it interesting that when Sarah started obeying Abraham, God gave them the son of promise, Isaac? Isaac means laughter. There was no laughter in that home until Sarah adapted. Abraham so loved her calm and gentle spirit that when she died at one-hundred-twenty-seven years of age, he cried and mourned for days. He was inconsolable.

It is only when a woman surrenders her life to her husband, reveres and worships him, and is willing to serve him, that she becomes really beautiful to him. She becomes a priceless jewel, the glory of femininity, his queen. I have not totally reached Sarah's advice, I would love to; but today's men don't want to be leaders. That is why God tells believers not to be un-equally yoked to un-believers. They wait on women to lead, and that is out of God's order. Every house hold's wife I talk to; the T V is the center of attraction. It comes first in most homes. Ann calls the remote control–Ramona. WT has grown up lots; and learned to control his temper. He's always been that man to go on trips with, to treat me like that special lady that I am. He is not controlling, I have always been free to be myself. We both had to learn we can not change anyone. Most men will tell us up front what they are about, we just don't listen; and then we try to change them. When we learn that no one can make us happy, we make ourselves happy; our expectations will change. It took years for me to learn that.

I refuse to let menopause change my life style. Glo said; "It should be call–The men-are-pausing". Not menopause "They are pausing to do what God told them to do". I am enjoying my life. I love sleeping late; I go to bed at no-clock-in- the morning. I do get my eight hours of sleep and rest. Ann being a nutritionist; tells me it's the sleep we get between 9: and 2: a.m. that helps the body to heal. I'm trying to change my habit. I have never been ill. I can see the bags coming under my eyes. I am the play mother to many young women all over in different states. They tell me they want to be like me when they grow up. People don't know what they might be asking; when they say they want to be like some one else; they don't have a clue what that person has gone through, or is going through to look like; or to be who they are. It takes lots of work and sacrifice. I teach them the positive things about life because I've lived it. I am told by many; that I resemble Tina Turner. I like hearing that. I love her as an entertainer; but I strive to look and be like who God wants me to be. My desire has been to meet Tina face to face some day. I have many of her DVD's. She takes great care of herself, it shows. My Grand daughter Reshae; has tried to get me on the Oprah show when she was having the ladies on who don't look their ages, she calls me her fabulous grand-mother. If we don't hurry up and get there I don't know how much longer I am going to look fabulous smile, that's ok as long as I am fabulous to God. He looks at the heart. God is blessing me to be getting on up in the mature age. He said He would re-new our youth as the Eagles if we obey Him. Oprah is my girl, she is a very objective talk show host, and she is fair with every one. I am waiting for my next dream to come true; which is the tummy tuck. I really do desire to have I have heard doctors say; because of past surgeries; exercises won't remove that flab. I've tried it for years and he is correct. Am I too old to want to have that type of surgery? One is not old because of age; it's all in your mind. I think it's my time now to do what I can to make me more beautiful. God has allowed me to live a long healthy life. I have much work to do for him. I would like to look and feel my best doing it

I am married and have eight children; the Grandma of five generations. I am an encourager, a friend and a wife. Not just married. I would like to say to my Husband; thank you for your patience and help while I spent so much time secluded writing this book. Thank you for growing up. I want my family to know how much I love you and appreciate you. Especially Ann who taught me all I know about the computer. She purchased the first one for me; and then all the girls together purchased a new one for me later Thanks to my extended family. Thanks to my sharp sister-in-law Mrs. Lewis for her advice. To my eight children, I never regretted raising you; there were tough times but never regret. You guys kept me young and on my feet. How you would tell me what looked nice on me, what I should wear or not to wear. Glo kept me coming to the school just because she wanted the kids to see her Mother. She would ask before going out the door to school what I was wearing that day; so she could cut up, and the teacher would have to call me to come to the School. Glo was always drawing and painting pictures for me.

Louise said; "she often think about the A.F.Hill Park; and how there was so much for them to do". What ever sports were offered there, they were asked to participate. It kept them busy. I never had to worry about where they were. Those activities taught them how to do a lot of good things; such as playing pool, kick ball, skating, running track, volley ball and swimming. They were kept busy. Maggie ran track in the relay races. No one could pass her up. She broke her ankle running. Louise said; those activities caused them to be better kids. She also said; "when they would go skating; she would change her clothes after leaving home and put on make up. Mickey would say; "you know Mama don't know you got that on". But she also said; "it always made her feel so relaxed to know I trusted her, to let her go places with other kids. She said; "they were so happy to get toys from the Salvation Army at Christmas time. I would buy them one new toy, something they could all share. That taught them to be sharing adults.

Glo and Jebez were the tattle tales. Glo would talk them into doing something, and then she would run and tell. She could talk her way out of a whipping. One night Jahari and I stepped out for an hour or two. We had just saved up enough money to put down on a new red couch and chair. The chair let into a bed. The arms were leather. Glo cut the arms of the chair with a razor blade, and caused everybody to get a whipping. I should have known she would be an Evangelist when she grew up; the way she could talk and convince me not to whip her.

Through it all everyone turned out to be productive being. Mickey Is a Grand Father and sings, Louise is a Grand Mother, a sub Teacher, in Real Estate, and was a home Day Care provider for several years. Jebez is a Grand Father, Play guitar and is a truck driver; Glo is a grand Mother, designer, Evangelist, Nurse's Assistance, and a Comedian. Maggie worked in finance as a Government Employer, a Grand mother, and a home Day Care provider. Ray is an Artist, Grand Mother, Pastor, has an Honorary Doctorate if Divinity and is raising her five Grand Children. Ann is Psalmist/Teacher/ Songwriter/Recording Artist and teaches Temple Maintenance. Since our temple belongs to God, She teaches how to keep it fit For Him to live in. Through Gods grace He has allowed WT and me to purchase another house, new and built from the ground. We repented and asked His forgiveness. He is another chance God.

My PRAYER

Dear God, I Thank you for the spiritual possessions you have given me through the experiences of my life. If it were not for the trials I have come through; the things I have experienced, done, and seen; the manifestations of your grace in my life, I would not be as spiritually rich as I am. I pray that I will be able to share my testimonies with others; that my life and my words would help to draw people to you; that I will be able to make a positive difference in someone's life because of what you have allowed me to experience and to share with others. Thank you for the lessons I have learned. Most of all, thank you for being there with me through it all and for carrying me so much of the way. In Jesus' name I pray. Amen